WHO KILLED GOLIATH?

Reading the Bible
with Heart and Mind

Edited by Robert F. Shedinger
and Deborah J. Spink

JUDSON PRESS
Valley Forge

Who Killed Goliath? Reading the Bible with Heart and Mind

Bible quotations in this volume are from:

The Holy Bible, King James Version. (KJV)

The New American Bible, copyright © 1970, 1986, 1991 by the Confraternity of Christian Doctrine, 3211 Fourth Street, N.E., Washington, DC 20017. All rights reserved. (NAB)

The New American Standard Bible, copyright © 1960, 1962, 1963, 1968, 1971, 1973, 1975, 1977 by the Lockman Foundation. Used by permission. (NASB)

HOLY BIBLE: *New International Version,* copyright © 1973, 1978, 1984. Used by permission of Zondervan Bible Publishers. (NIV)

The New Jerusalem Bible, copyright © 1985 by Darton, Longman & Todd, Ltd. and Doubleday, a division of Random House, Inc. Reprinted by permission. (NJB)

The New King James Version, copyright © 1972, 1984 by Thomas Nelson, Inc. (NKJV)

The Holy Bible, New Living Translation, copyright © 1996. Used by permission of Tyndale House Publishers, Inc., Wheaton, IL 60189. All rights reserved. (NLT)

The New Revised Standard Version of the Bible, copyright © 1989 by the Division of Christian Education of the National Council of the Churches of Christ in the United States of America. Used by permission. All rights reserved. (NRSV)

Library of Congress Cataloging-in-Publication Data

Who killed Goliath? : reading the Bible with heart and mind / edited by Robert F. Shedinger and Deborah J. Spink.
     p. cm.
   ISBN 0-8170-1374-1 (pbk. : alk. paper)
   1. Bible—Hermeneutics. I. Shedinger, Robert F. II. Spink, Deborah J.
   BS476.W478   2001
   220.6'01—dc21   00-060335

Printed in the U.S.A.

07 06 05 04 03 02 01

10 9 8 7 6 5 4 3 2 1

WHO KILLED
GOLIATH?

This book has been written in honor of Dr. Glenn A. Koch and Dr. Thomas F. McDaniel, who for more than thirty years were the mainstay of the biblical studies department at Eastern Baptist Theological Seminary in Wynnewood, Pennsylvania. All of the contributors to this volume at some point in their careers studied under Drs. Koch and McDaniel at Eastern, where they were taught not to be afraid to ask critical questions about the biblical text and to fully engage their minds as well as their hearts in their study, interpretation, and proclamation of the Scriptures. To them we dedicate this book, and we pray that in some small way each chapter is a way of saying thanks to them, and to all our teachers, who have dedicated their lives to the educating of future pastors, scholars, and teachers.

CONTENTS

INTRODUCTION

In August of 1999 Buford Furrow walked into a Jewish community center in Los Angeles and began shooting at defenseless children whose only crime was being Jewish and wanting to have fun at a summer day camp. Later, he allegedly killed a Filipino American postal worker for no reason other than the postal worker was not a white European American. Furrow's actions, unfortunately, were not unique; we have all too frequently been faced in recent years with violence perpetrated against certain groups in America by those adhering to extremist, white supremacist views. What we frequently do not realize, however, is that at least some members of the white supremacy movement in America turn to the Bible to find support for these extremist views.

In Numbers 25 the Bible relates the story of a man named Phinehas, who upon seeing an Israelite man bringing a Midianite woman into the congregation of Israel, takes a spear and pierces the man and the woman, killing them. Because of his brave action in protecting the Israelites from the potentially corrupting influence of a foreign woman, Phinehas is given praise by God, and he and his descendants are promised a perpetual priesthood in return for his great zeal for God.

This seemingly innocuous story, buried in an often overlooked book of the Old Testament, has, not surprisingly, become the rallying point for many members of the white supremacy movement. Seeing themselves as inheritors of the Phinehas priesthood promised by God in Numbers, people like Buford Furrow place themselves in the role of Phinehas, while members of other religious or ethnic groups are cast in the role of the Midianite woman. Since Phinehas is praised by God for murdering the Midianite woman in the biblical account, white supremacists believe it is their God-ordained duty to exterminate all those not of a white European descent.

Most people would, of course, see this interpretation of the Bible as entirely wrong and antithetical to anything intended by God or the original authors. But on what grounds can we offer an alternative interpretation? The Phinehas Priesthood movement among white supremacists in this country is, to be sure, an extreme example of what can happen when one interprets the Bible in a strictly literal or superficial sense. But in this biblical text God does praise Phinehas for killing a man and his non-Israelite partner, and this does, at least on the surface, seem to support the idea that God wants us to adopt a violently intolerant attitude toward those not like ourselves. The obvious question must be asked: Is it possible to understand Numbers 25 as divinely inspired and authoritative but not as giving divine legitimacy to attitudes of violent intolerance? We believe the answer to this question is a resounding yes, and that the problem with the white supremacists' interpretation of Numbers 25 stems from its superficial nature. It is our contention that the Bible is a complex and profound vehicle of revelation, and that its divine nature is best encountered when we go below the surface and engage in readings of its texts that take us beyond simplistic, literal interpretations. It is, therefore, the purpose of this book to introduce you to a variety of different strategies for reading the Bible in a deeper and more complex way, and to demonstrate the way in which these different interpretive strategies influence the theological messages we receive when we turn to the Bible.

What we are proposing, in other words, is a hermeneutical grid for use in interpreting the biblical text, a hermeneutical grid quite different from the one most people ordinarily use. A hermeneutical grid is a set of fundamental assumptions we hold about the nature of the Bible, assumptions so foundational to our understanding that frequently we hold them without even realizing it. When we read the Bible, everything gets filtered through this set of assumptions so that certain types of interpretations will automatically be filtered out before they are even considered. For example, some people read the Bible through the hermeneutical grid of literality; that is, they assume that the Bible is a book that everywhere relays an accurate, literal account of what happened in the past. When the Bible is read in this way, nonliteral ways of understanding the text will never even be considered; the hermeneutical grid of literality will have already filtered them out.

We believe that the Bible itself challenges the validity of any hermeneutical grid that allows only literal or superficial readings of the text. While we do not question that there are parts of the biblical story that are literally and historically accurate, parts that will yield themselves to literal or surface readings, there are many other parts of the Bible that can be characterized only as places of tension. That is, there are places where what the Bible says in one place seems to contradict what it says in another, as well as places where what the Bible says seems to contradict life as we experience it. For an example of the second type of tension, consider the creation story in Genesis, where the idea of a seven-day creation comes into conflict with modern scientific understandings of a universe billions of years old. Or consider the stories in Genesis of people who live unimaginably long periods of time—one thousand years in the case of Methuselah—in contrast to our experience of a human life expectancy of about eight decades. There are many examples of biblical texts that are internally inconsistent or inconsistent with our own life experience, leading us to the question of whether these texts are intended to be read in a literal, superficial way. The Bible itself seems to drive us beneath the surface into a search for more complex readings and the more profound theological messages that will inevitably come with them.

When faced with these kinds of biblical tensions, there are two main approaches that people normally take, neither of which we find very satisfying. One approach is to ignore the tensions, to pretend that they are not there, and continue on, treating the Bible as a simple text whose message can be appropriated via superficial interpretations. We find this method unsatisfying because it is dishonest. The tensions are there; they cannot be ignored. To ignore them is to force the Bible to conform to a preconceived understanding of our own making, rather than allowing the Bible to dictate its true nature to us. If we accept the Bible as in some sense God's revelation to us, we must be willing to humble ourselves before it and allow it to dictate its nature to us no matter how difficult or disturbing we find that nature to be. To do otherwise means subordinating the Bible's message to our needs and has the effect of placing us as arbiters over God's Word, which makes a travesty out of the idea of revelation.

The other approach is to take the tensions so seriously that we lose all respect for and interest in the Bible as a source of divine revelation. This is the approach that atheists and other critics of organized Christianity frequently follow. They grab hold of all of the tensions and contradictions in the Bible as if tensions were all that existed in this book, and then they argue that these tensions and contradictions render the Bible useless and meaningless. For example, one of the outstanding critics of organized Christianity was Thomas Paine, an influential thinker of the American Revolution. In 1794 Paine published his tract *The Age of Reason,* which included a detailed critique of the Bible in which Paine painstakingly pointed out every possible contradiction he could find. Having done this, he concluded, "The contradictory impossibilities contained in the Old Testament and the New put them in the case of a man who swears for and against. Either evidence convicts him of perjury, and equally destroys reputation."

We do not think that Paine did destroy the reputation of the Bible. Like so many critics of the Bible, Paine considered only the tensions while ignoring virtually all else, and it is clear that he did not become a critic of the church as a result of his critique of the Bible. Rather, he had already come into conflict with the church and was merely criticizing the Bible to give legitimacy to his already developed negativity toward the church. Paine was more honest about the tensions than many Christians have been, but his approach to the Bible as a whole remains simplistic and unsatisfying.

Rather than ignoring biblical tensions or seeing them as evidence of the Bible's utter uselessness as Scripture, we want to propose a third alternative. It is our conviction that tensions and contradictions in the Bible are evidence of nothing more than that the Bible is a complex—not a simple—piece of literature, and that its revelatory message must be appropriated via deeper and more profound ways of reading. Just as Paul exhorted the Romans to a renewing of their minds, we want to encourage you to begin reading the Bible with both your heart and your mind.

But what does it mean to read the Bible with one's mind? There is no easy answer to this question. But we believe it means getting below the surface of the biblical text and seeing it as a multifaceted diamond; it sparkles in different ways, depending on the angle of one's view. Getting below the surface means approaching the Bible in more than one way and being open to allowing the Bible to show us the variety of ways that it can be read and interpreted. The essays in this book do just that. In each one the author takes a slightly different approach to understanding a particular biblical text, and in each case the author offers an interpretation of that text different, and sometimes radically so, from the traditional interpretations that most Christians are accustomed to. We hope and expect that in reading these essays you will develop many new insights into familiar biblical texts, insights that will lead you on your own journey to a deeper appreciation of God's Word than can be gained from any number of simplistic guides or how-to books addressing biblical interpretation that are currently on the market.

We begin in chapter 1 with Robert Parkinson's plea for the church to take seriously the textual history of the Bible. The books of the Bible exist in thousands of ancient manuscripts, most of which have been discovered only in the last century, and no two of which are identical. The irony is that just at the time when this plethora of new manuscripts is available, the textual history of the Bible is being ignored in churches and even in seminaries. Parkinson calls for this situation to be reversed and demonstrates the relevance of the Bible's textual history for Christian proclamation. Parkinson believes that the textual history of the Bible is not a subject for academics only, but one that is crucial for ordinary Christians as well.

In chapter 2 Grant H. Ward looks at two words found in the creation accounts from the book of Genesis that deal with the issue of the relationship between men and women. He challenges the accepted translations of these words as they are found in most English Bibles, and shows how alternative meanings for these words, meanings attested in the standard biblical Hebrew lexicon, can dramatically alter the interpretation of the biblical text and consequently the influence that the text has had, particularly on the role of women throughout history.

In chapter 3 Robert F. Shedinger engages in a close reading of the familiar David and Goliath story, showing that the biblical narrative is fraught with textual and literary problems that call into question the historical reliability of the whole account. By taking these textual and literary issues seriously, Shedinger suggests that David in fact never did kill Goliath, an idea that leads Shedinger to appropriate a theological message from this narrative quite different from the one most Christians have learned in Sunday school and church.

In chapter 4 Deborah J. Spink considers another aspect of the literary nature of the Bible, the idea of genre. Specifically, she considers the literary genre of the lament, which she studies in its biblical and its ancient Mesopotamian forms. She finds three characteristics of the lament genre that she also finds in use in a present-day situation of lament as it occurred in 1989 to a church congregation in Topeka, Kansas. Spink sees a tremendous irony in the fact that churches are removing biblical laments from their liturgies when in fact contemporary congregations lament in much the same way as the ancient biblical communities. She ends with a call for the church to return the biblical lament to its liturgical traditions.

The consideration of textual and literary issues in the Bible is important but, by itself, insufficient. One must also look to the historical and theological context out of which the biblical texts arose. This is what Benjamin G. Wright does in chapter 5 with his discussion of heaven as a place of revelation. Wright contends that the familiar concept of heaven as a final resting place of eternal reward for the righteous is actually not found in the Bible, but is the product of later Christian interpretation. Looking at references to heaven as it appears in the letters of Paul and the book of Revelation, Wright demonstrates how these references can be fully understood only when they are seen against the background of contemporary views on heaven. Thus, Wright introduces us to several Jewish works from the years just before New Testament times in which the concept of heaven plays a major role. Looked at in this way, the concept of heaven in the New Testament means something quite different from our common Christian understanding of it.

Along with textual, literary, and historical issues, it is also important to inquire into the sociological background of biblical texts. Thus, in chapter 6 Terence C. Mournet employs sociological analysis to recreate the honor/shame structure that stands behind Paul's first letter to the Corinthians. Mournet argues that when the social structure of Corinthian society is rightly understood, Paul's letter to the Corinthian church can be read as Paul's appeal to the Corinthian church to work for the reversal of the dominant honor/shame system. Mournet offers numerous insights into the full meaning of Paul's words that are lost when those words are not read against the backdrop of the social structure of the society Paul is addressing, and this sharpens the focus of Paul's appeal for the church today.

Using a similar strategy along with modern feminist inquiry, Julia Pizzuto-Pomaco, in chapter 7, considers the diversity of race, class, and gender relationships that existed in the early Christian church as evidenced by a close reading of Romans 16. Pizzuto-Pomaco makes the compelling argument that when read in this way, Romans 16, which is frequently ignored as nothing more than an appendix to the "more important" chapters of Romans, becomes a text infused with deep historical and theological insights that are every bit as important as the so-called body of the letter, and which carry an equally profound message for the church today.

While it is always important to consider the context surrounding the biblical text, as the previous essays do in one way or another, one must also take into account the history of the interpretation of a text. How has a text been understood by Christians in the centuries before our time, and how are our understandings dependent upon this interpretive tradition? Karen L. Onesti takes up this question in chapter 8, where she surveys what she sees as a pervasive inherited tradition of misinterpretation as it applies to the traditions concerning Mary Magdalene, the Samaritan woman, and the woman caught in adultery. Onesti forces us to consider why our traditional understandings have led to a vilification of these women, especially when there does not seem to be any biblical support for such vilification.

In a somewhat different way Robert L. Manzinger, in chapter 9, uses a later theological tradition in a positive way to illuminate and nuance the famous dictum of Jesus to "love your neighbor as yourself." Specifically, Manzinger turns to the work of the Jewish ethical thinker Emmanuel Levinas and his understanding of an interpersonal ethic. Manzinger argues that devotional knowledge of God must be linked to ethical action and that ethical action as defined by Jesus and seen through the eyes of Levinas applies to every person ("the other," "the enemy") we meet. In this way, Manzinger shows us the importance of engaging in deep reflection on the meaning of a biblical text rather than being satisfied with a simple, surface reading.

Finally, in a concluding postscript, we will begin the process of considering how these different reading strategies can be brought to bear on the text of Numbers 25. How might we see God being revealed in this text when we read it in a deeper way? We will not attempt to give a comprehensive answer to this question but merely indicate the direction in which such an answer may be found, and to invite you, the reader, to begin reflecting more deeply on this text yourself.

The Bible is a complex text, and thus its message can be truly appropriated only when we take its various complexities into account in our reading. We believe that this is what it means to read the Bible with heart and mind, and we invite you now to engage your mind as you begin your journey through this book. While we do not promise that your journey will always be easy (doing so would defeat our purpose), we do guarantee that it will be enlightening.

CHAPTER 1

New Testament Textual Criticism

Don't Leave the Church without It!

ROBERT PARKINSON

The most reliable manuscripts of Mark's Gospel end at 16:8: "They said nothing to anyone, for they were afraid." Yet, you are more likely to hear a sermon on the interpolated verse 15, "Go into the whole world and proclaim the good news to the whole creation," than on the strange ending at verse 8. Such is the disregard for textual criticism in the life of the church. Lectionaries are helping to correct the problem by including the reading of Mark 16:1–8 on Easter Sunday in Year B, and sermons to go with the reading are now appearing in print.[1] Nevertheless, in many congregations (in most, I would suggest) preachers and ministers routinely read and preach from the long ending of Mark and other secondary texts without the slightest mention of their being secondary and without any reference to the history of the text.

Perhaps ministers are unaware of the textual issues involved. It is quite possible now to graduate from a respected seminary with no knowledge of the biblical languages and no capacity to handle a critical commentary or apparatus. Some graduates may struggle even to evaluate the marginal notes in the most popular editions of the English Bible. Textual criticism, and to a lesser degree Greek and Hebrew, have been eclipsed by subjects and disciplines deemed more important, relevant, necessary, or imaginative. In church and seminary New Testament textual criticism is becoming a lost art, and this at just such a time when important new perspectives are revitalizing the discipline from within.

Even where seminaries continue to equip their students with the tools for biblical exegesis, some of their graduates, upon entering the ministry, act as though what they learned in seminary is of little or no practical use in gospel ministry. Thus, preachers perpetuate false notions about the text of the Bible and maintain their congregations in blissful ignorance.[2]

The publication of the Bible as a one-volume printed English text, while a marvelous benefit to the life of the church, may also be part of the problem. It creates the illusion that there is a single and unchangeable text. Before the invention of printing, it was self-evident that the text of the Bible was preserved in handwritten manuscripts that sometimes differed significantly from each other. Today, many readers of the Bible have no knowledge of how the Bible came into being or any awareness of the prior existence of Scripture as a manuscript tradition. When individuals learn that no New Testament manuscript has exactly the same text as any other, they are often surprised and experience their new learning as a serious challenge to their faith.

The problem addressed by biblical text critics is that the original documents upon which our Bible is based no longer exist. The actual products of the biblical authors perished long ago, and we now rely on handwritten copies of copies of the original autographs. What is more, these copies evidence various differences as both conscious and unconscious changes were introduced by scribes through the centuries of replication. Textual criticism attempts to account for the differences and explain how or why changes occurred, thus establishing which readings are primary and which are secondary. Many have thought that such a process can provide for us a *New Testament in the Original Greek*.[3]

So great is the confidence in this venture that it has become axiomatic to define the task of New Testament textual criticism entirely along the lines of recovering the original autographs. *Harper's Bible Dictionary* is representative when it maintains that the aim of biblical textual criticism is "to establish the original wording or form of the biblical text insofar as this is possible."[4] When looked at in this way, textual criticism is the most foundational of the fields of biblical study.

Formerly known by the unfortunate epithet "lower criticism," it attempts to furnish a text without which no further investigation could be carried out. One might think that this would ensure it pride of place among the biblical disciplines. Not at all! Its own importance has contributed to its neglect. Seen as the sole domain of specialists, the preserve of a select few, it seems to admit no room for participation from the rest of us.

The foundational nature of textual criticism has contributed to its neglect also because it leads one to assume that the work has already been done. We now have, in the scholarly editions of the Greek New Testament, a so-called standard text. This, plus the advent of modern English translations such as the NIV and NRSV, has led some scholars and probably many more teachers, students, and pastors to assume that the text is sure. The textual critics have done their work; we can get on with the more imaginative task of interpretation.

If only it were so simple. The fact is that textual criticism is itself an interpretative discipline. The text critic does not simply establish the text and then get out of the way. Rather, his or her conclusions are arrived at by combining the insights gained from manuscript analysis with those from other disciplines such as literary, rhetorical, and historical criticism.

This is particularly true with the criterion for evaluating textual variants known as "intrinsic probability." Here, various aspects such as the author's style and use of language, the context of the passage, and historical questions regarding the Christian community and its influence on the text are taken into account. Sometimes these offer important keys to our understanding of a text's history.

Take Mark 16, for example. Text critics long ago reached a consensus that "the earliest ascertainable form of the Gospel of Mark ended with 16:8."[5] There were still, however, considerable problems. Why would anybody end a Gospel with women stunned into silence at the discovery of the empty tomb? Why are there no resurrection appearances? Why does verse 8 ignore the rules of grammar and break off in the middle of a sentence, ending with the Greek particle *gar* ("therefore").

Various solutions have been suggested. Perhaps the author died before the Gospel could be completed or, as Bruce Metzger thought most probable, "the Gospel accidentally lost its last leaf before it was multiplied by transcription."[6] Newer literary considerations point in the direction of authorial intent. Robert M. Fowler, for example, finds in Mark "an abundance of irony, ambiguity and mystery."[7] The abrupt and puzzling ending is thoroughly in keeping with Mark's approach throughout. "Matthew likes to tell us what to think, Mark wants us to learn for ourselves."[8] The Gospel of Mark is unfinished, then, only in the sense that it invites its readers to enter into the story and complete it in their own experience. Manuscript evidence combined with insights from literary criticism has significantly advanced our understanding of Mark 16:1–8. Here, as elsewhere, the tasks of establishing, describing, and understanding the text are all part of the text-critical endeavor.

Can textual criticism deliver a "New Testament in the original Greek"? There are at least two reasons why we should seriously doubt it. The first has to do with the materials and methods at our disposal. Even with the great papyri discoveries of the twentieth century we are unable to get back beyond the second century. Moreover, the papyri evidence points to a multiform tradition at this early period. The vast majority of textual variants had already been created. The New Testament documents were being transmitted independently of one another, and no ecclesiastical control was exercised over the text. Scribes felt free to conform their text to that of other manuscripts, biblical passages, or to their own understanding. "During the second century in particular . . . scribal errors proliferated."[9] The existence of a great number of variant readings at the very earliest time means that in many instances we simply cannot be sure of the original text.

The second reason concerns the nature of the biblical documents. David C. Parker suggests that it is unlikely that the Gospels, for example, are the kinds of texts that have originals as such.[10] That is to say that in all likelihood, like many classical music scores or theatrical scripts, from the very moment they appeared, the Gospels underwent revision of one sort or another. Perhaps the Gospels themselves were issued in multiple forms, as the authors, redactors, or communities that produced them found cause to tweak them, add to them, and clarify them.

None of this is to say that we cannot or should not attempt to get back to as ancient and reliable a text as possible or to distinguish between primary and secondary readings. It is to suggest, however, that we should always be open to the possibility of different but equally viable readings, and that where derivative readings can be accounted for, we do well to attend to the story they tell. The work of scholars such as Bart Ehrman in the United States and David C. Parker in Great Britain has brought new attention to this aspect of the critical discipline.[11]

Readings tell their own stories. Variations in the text reveal the theological struggles and discoveries of religious communities. They show us which aspects of the tradition became edifying and which became troublesome to particular people in particular circumstances. They reveal the human tendency to make the Scripture fit one's theology, and they reveal the power of Scripture to keep reasserting itself against attempts to "correct" it. They bear witness to competing ideas, theologies, and doctrines. When we pay attention to this information we learn about God and about the human condition, we learn about religious communities and their histories, we learn about the Spirit who sustained those communities, and we learn about ourselves. When we pay attention to these stories we engage in theology. We can often learn as much then from the apparatus at the foot of the page as we can from the body of a critical edition of the biblical text.

When preachers first sit down to study their text they do well to pay attention to variant readings. If they are able to read New Testament Greek, they can consult the apparatus in their edition of the text. If not, a critical commentary will identify and discuss instances of textual variation. All this is important and helpful because significant variants reveal the aspects of any given text that have been problematic through the years. They provide fertile ground for reflection. Why did some of our forebears find it necessary to insert this or omit that? Might this be an area of continuing concern or an aspect that warrants further investigation? Are there ideas embraced or rejected by this reading that might inform my preaching? These and similar questions can provide grist for the preacher's mill.

Ministers and preachers might also consider reading and preaching occasionally from the text of a specific manuscript rather than from the composite text in our Greek New Testament. This might remind congregations that the various manuscripts themselves functioned as Scripture for the communities that produced or preserved them. If the readings do not seem to come from our Bible, they do come from what was someone's Bible; and if they are not authoritative to us, they once were authoritative to someone. I will never forget the impact of Dr. Thomas McDaniel reading and preaching from a translation of Shem Tob's Hebrew Gospel of Matthew during my years at Eastern Baptist Theological Seminary.[12] It breathed new life into an old text and suggested new possibilities for interpretation and understanding. Just to hear it read was a profound and thought-provoking experience. Perhaps more of us should read pertinent passages from the text of a particular manuscript that preserves interesting, helpful, or possibly more authentic readings.

Granted, it may not always be easy to find such a text, but some of the major Greek manuscripts are available in whole or part as published collations, facsimiles, or even translations. When a full text is unavailable, it may be possible to reconstruct a particular passage from the information contained in apparatuses and commentaries. At the very least the reader might choose to omit verses enclosed by double brackets in versions of the English Bible or those that the marginal notes indicate as doubtful.

The last three chapters of Luke's Gospel in the Greek manuscript known as Codex Bezae are considerably different from those found in our English Bibles. The great textual critics Westcott and Hort thought them more authentic, and although their view has been severely challenged, it has, I think, been successfully vindicated by the work of Bart Ehrman and David Parker.[13] The preacher could read the last chapters of Luke from the shorter version suggested by the marginal notes, omitting the angelic assistance in the garden and the sweating of great drops of blood, keeping to the shorter text of the Last Supper, and dropping the apparent harmonizations with the Gospel of John in the resurrection appearance of Luke 24:36–43. A shorter, sharper story with different theological ramifications emerges, but plenty still remains for the preacher to work on.

Preachers can make imaginative and instructive use of textual variants in their sermons. An inductive, "questing" technique might be used, where the preacher introduces a reading and examines the alternatives one after the other, weighing pros and cons before arriving at the chosen reading as a climax to the sermon.[14] It is not always necessary to arrive at a "correct" reading. The preacher may let the advantages and disadvantages of different readings hang delicately in the balance and allow the hearer to decide. On the other hand, the preacher may believe that, in one instance or another, it is not a case of either/or but of both/and.

Mark 1:41 can serve as an example. Here, in the prelude to Jesus' cleansing of the leper, some manuscripts have Jesus "filled with compassion" and others have him "filled with anger." It is difficult to decide which reading has the greater claim to authenticity. "Compassion" has impressive manuscript support. It is much easier, however, to see why "anger" might be changed to "compassion" than why "compassion" might ever be replaced with "anger." A preacher could certainly make something of both readings, exploring why Christ might have compassion on the sick and why he might be angry with his opponents or with the very powers of sickness and disease. There is gospel to be proclaimed in both readings, and if the preacher believes there is also a story about the church's tendency to domesticate Christ, forcing him into more comfortable categories, then this story also might be told.

If preachers are to tell such stories, they will need to develop their text-critical skills. Some suggest that this is beyond the capacity of the average minister and is therefore an elitist request. Nothing could be further from the truth. Some knowledge of the biblical languages would be a great advantage, to be sure, but a basic course in Greek and Hebrew tools would provide enough for most. A course on biblical textual criticism would benefit the preacher immensely, but where such is not available, the interested reader can go far on the recognized handbooks in the field.[15] After all, ministers are not usually seeking expert status in the fields that inform their ministry. Literary theory and hermeneutics, for example, can be every bit as arcane as textual criticism, yet we expect preachers to make use of these subjects. The greater danger is not that of elitism but that of expecting too little from our ministers and preachers. Anyone capable of standing up before a congregation and delivering a cogent message is probably more than capable of learning a few skills in the neglected discipline of textual criticism.

I close with a simple plea, that seminaries and ministers and even laypersons pay more attention to the text-critical study of the Bible, for too many of our congregations have no knowledge of the manuscript tradition. Thus, a rather wooden view of Scripture has developed that seems to rely on the supposition that the Bible was written in English and printed in heaven. Individuals and faith communities grow spiritually when they interact with Scripture, when they enter into conversation with the tradition, interpreting and reinterpreting the Word for new contexts and situations. Textual criticism provides exciting opportunities for just this kind of interaction. It is neglected only to the detriment of the church.[16]

Questions for Further Reflection and Discussion

1. Do you think that biblical textual criticism is neglected in the church? Do you think that this is good or bad for the church?

2. What is it about the Bible that makes it authoritative? Why do you experience it as inspired? Where does the power of its message come from?

3. Does the fact that the Gospels began to change from the moment they were written affect your view of their inspiration? If so, in what way?

4. Is it possible that the Spirit was at work in the development as well as in the creation of the biblical documents, and continues to be at work in our attempts to interpret and appropriate the Scriptures for today?

Endnotes

1. C. S. Rodd offers an illuminating sermon on Mark 16:1–8 that makes exemplary use of literary and text-critical insights in *The Expository Times* 111, no. 6 (March 2000): 203–4. Resources for preaching on Mark 16:1–8 can be found in Fred B. Craddock, John H. Hayes, Carl R. Holladay, and Gene M. Tucker, *Preaching through the Christian Year: Year B* (Valley Forge, Pa.: Trinity Press International, 1993).

2. Admittedly, this problem reaches to all aspects of academic study. At the time of this writing a very promising series, "In Honesty of Preaching," has begun in *The Expository Times*. It examines the relationship of academic study and preaching and begins in the April 2000 issue (vol. 111, no. 7).

3. The title of the Greek Testament of Westcott and Hort, 1881.

4. Paul J. Achtemeier, ed., *Harper's Bible Dictionary* (San Francisco: Harper and Row, 1985), 129.

5. Bruce M. Metzger, *A Textual Commentary on the Greek New Testament*, corr. ed. (Stuttgart: United Bible Societies, 1975), 126.

6. Ibid., 126 n. 7.

7. Robert M. Fowler, "Reader-Response Criticism: Figuring Mark's Reader," in Janice Capel Anderson and Stephen D. Moore, eds., *Mark and Method: New Approaches in Biblical Studies* (Minneapolis: Fortress Press, 1992), 78.

8. Ibid., 79.

9. Gordon G. Fee, "Textual Criticism of the New Testament," in Eldon J. Epp and Gordon D. Fee, *Studies in the Theory and Method of New Testament Textual Criticism* (Grand Rapids: Eerdmans, 1993), 9.

10. See David C. Parker, *The Living Text of the Gospels* (Cambridge: Cambridge University Press, 1997), esp. pp. 1–7.

11. See Bart D. Ehrman, "The Text as Window: New Testament Manuscripts and the Social History of Early Christianity," in Bart D. Ehrman and Michael W. Holmes, eds., *The Text of the New Testament in Contemporary Research* (Grand Rapids: Eerdmans, 1995), 361–79; idem, *The Orthodox Corruption of Scripture* (New York and Oxford: Oxford University Press, 1993); Parker, *Living Text of the Gospels*.

12. George Howard, *The Gospel of Matthew According to a Primitive Hebrew Text* (Macon, Ga.: Mercer University Press, 1987).

13. See Ehrman, *Orthodox Corruption of Scripture,* and Parker, *Living Text of the Gospels*.

14. James W. Cox uses the term "questing" for sermons that raise questions and invite the congregation to join in the process of seeking possible answers. See Cox's *Preaching,* 2nd ed. (San Francisco, Harper and Row, 1993), 162–64.

15. I particularly recommend the following: Kurt Aland and Barbara Aland, *The Text of the New Testament,* trans. Erroll F. Rhodes, 2nd ed. (Grand Rapids: Eerdmans; Leiden: Brill, 1989); Bruce M. Metzger, *The Text of the New Testament: Its Transmission, Corruption, and Restoration,* 3rd ed. (Oxford and New York: Oxford University Press, 1992); Léon Vaganay and Christian-Bernard Amphoux, *An Introduction to New Testament Textual Criticism,* trans. Jenny Heimerdinger (Cambridge: Cambridge University Press, 1991); and, of course, Parker's *Living Text of the Gospels* and Ehrman's *Orthodox Corruption of Scripture*.

16. Drs. Koch and McDaniel always treated the text and its history seriously and sought to bridge the gap between study and pulpit by careful exegesis,

credible interpretation, and honest communication. Thus, their courses on Greek and Hebrew never lost sight of the texts to which the languages related. Text-critical issues were raised naturally and by way of fascinating story and lively illustration in the process of teaching their students to read the biblical languages. The further introduction to New Testament textual criticism offered by Dr. Koch and by the seminar on Shem Tob's Hebrew Gospel of Matthew by Dr. McDaniel were exceptional among seminary offerings at the Master of Divinity level. Modules such as these alerted me to some of the issues and possibilities of the much neglected discipline of biblical (and, for me, particularly New Testament) textual criticism.

CHAPTER 2

Two Words (and Their Translations) That Have Indeed Hurt[1]

GRANT H. WARD

I can remember as a child repeating numerous times (almost always in the situation where the person who has just hurled the words at me was much bigger than I), "Sticks and stones may break my bones but words will never hurt me." I had not learned then the ways in which words and their interpretations could hurt much more deeply than sticks and stones. This was also the case in many of the churches to which I belonged as I was growing up in the South, and continues to be the case in many churches today as traditional understandings and translations of words from the Bible in its original languages continue to hurt certain groups in the church.

In this essay I argue that the translations of two words, one from the second creation account[2] in Genesis 2 and the other from the description of the punishments meted out to Adam and Eve in Genesis 3 for their disobedience, have been used to support interpretations of those texts which, despite the best attempts of many biblical scholars to interpret these texts in alternative ways, have continued to be used to justify the superiority of men in a large segment of the Christian church, and have indeed hurt and have been painful for women in their struggle for equality within the Christian church.

During the 1997 meeting of the Southern Baptist Convention in Dallas this motion was made: "That the President of the Southern Baptist Convention appoint a committee to review *The Baptist Faith and Message* of May 9, 1963, for the primary purpose of adding an Article on The Family, and to bring the amendment to the next convention for approval." In response, Convention president Thomas D. Elliff appointed The Baptist Faith and Message Study Committee, which presented a motion to the Southern Baptist Convention in Salt Lake City in 1998. The motion passed on June 9. The following paragraph from the motion concerns the wife's duty to "submit graciously" to her husband. Among the proof texts cited in support are Genesis 1:26–28; 2:18–25; 3:1–20.

> The husband and wife are of equal worth before God, since both are created in God's image. The marriage relationship models the way God relates to His people. A husband is to love his wife as Christ loved the church. He has the God-given responsibility to provide for, to protect, and to lead his family. A wife is to submit herself graciously to the servant leadership of her husband even as the church willingly submits to the headship of Christ. She, being in the image of God as is her husband and thus equal to him, has the God-given responsibility to respect her husband and to *serve as his helper* in managing the household and nurturing the next generation.[3]

While the statement does at least admit that women are created "in the image of God," somehow the conclusion is still reached that it is the wife who "is to submit herself graciously to the servant leadership of her husband" and "to serve as his helper" in managing the household and nurturing the next generation (how ironic such a statement must seem to the many women who would be glad if they could get any help from their husbands in these tasks!). At the last meeting of the Southern Baptist Convention (arguably still the largest Protestant denomination in the United States), according to Adrian Rogers, who chairs The Baptist Faith and Message Committee, "The convention had spoken clearly its conviction that while both men and women are gifted and called for ministry, the office of pastor is limited to men as qualified by Scripture."[4]

Here follow quotations from Tony Evans, one of the prominent members of Promise Keepers, a Christian men's organization that is growing rapidly in membership as a result of holding mass rallies around the United States in the last few years.

> Don't you understand, mister, you are royalty and God has chosen you to be priest of your home?
> . . . sit down with your wife and say something like this, "Honey, I've made a terrible mistake. . . . I gave up leading this family, and I forced you to take my place. Now I must reclaim that role." . . . I'm not suggesting you ask for your role back, I'm urging you to take it back . . . there can be no compromise here. If you're going to lead, you must lead. . . . Treat the lady gently and lovingly. But lead![5]

And Jerry Falwell, in praise of the organization, offered these words: "It appears that America's anti-Biblical feminist movement is at last dying, thank God, and is possibly being replaced by a Christ-centered men's movement." One might argue that throughout much of the history of the church, the church has primarily been a "men's movement," at least in terms of positions of authority within it. This sort of justification for the authority of men has often been based on the interpretation of several passages from Genesis 2 and 3 and the translation of several key words contained therein.

'Ezer in Genesis 2:18 and 2:20

Here, with italics added, is the text of Genesis 2:5–8,18–23 in the NRSV.

> [5]When no plant of the field was yet in the earth and no herb of the field had yet sprung up—for the Lord God had not caused it to rain upon the earth, and there was no one to till the ground; [6]but a stream would rise from the earth, and water the whole face of the ground— [7]then the Lord God formed man from the dust of the ground, and breathed into his nostrils the breath of life; and the man became a living being. [8]And the Lord God planted a garden in Eden, in the east; and there he put the man whom he had formed. . . . [18]Then the Lord God said, "It is not good that the man should be alone; I will make him *a helper as his partner.*" [19]So out of the ground the Lord God formed every animal of the field and every bird of the air, and brought them to the man to see what he would call them; and whatever the man called every living creature, that was its name. [20]The man gave names to all cattle, and to the birds of the air, and to every animal of the field;

but for the man there was not found a *helper as his partner.* [21]So the Lord God caused a deep sleep to fall upon the man, and he slept; then he took one of his ribs and closed up its place with flesh. [22]And the rib that the Lord God had taken from the man he made into a woman and brought her to the man. [23]Then the man said, "This at last is bone of my bones and flesh of my flesh; this one shall be called Woman, for out of Man this one was taken."

In the Hebrew text the phrase "helper as his partner" in Genesis 2:18 and 20 is *'ezer k^eneg^edo,* and it has been translated in various ways but almost always with some sense of the woman as "helper." After looking at the meaning of *'ezer* in the Hebrew lexicon,[6] at other passages in the Bible where the same word is used, and in the narrative here in Genesis 2, one might wish to question the validity of retaining the idea of "helper," given the understanding of the meaning of this word in current English usage.

This second creation account in Genesis, beginning at 2:4, portrays God as being concerned that Adam is alone and deciding to, as the King James Version translates the Hebrew phrase, "make a *help meet* for him." God then makes all the creatures of creation, but "there was not found a *help meet* for him." In verse 21, after putting Adam into a deep sleep, God creates the female to fulfill this role. The Hebrew behind these words (*'ezer* as a *neged*) has been translated in various ways in recent translations of the Bible. Besides the KJV "help meet,"[7] both the NIV and the NAB have "helper suitable for him," while the NRSV and the NAB have introduced the idea of partnership in translating these words. The NRSV has "I will make him a helper as his partner," while the NAB has "I will make a suitable partner for him." The NLT translates, "I will make a companion who will help him," and the NKJV, "I will make him a helper comparable to him."[8] The idea of woman as helper comes in the various translations of *'ezer* as "helper."

However, while the Hebrew lexicon does have "help" as one of the meanings for this word, it does not easily lend itself to the meaning of "helper" in the sense of one who is not equal. Despite the various recent translations, which have moved toward some sense of equality with the use of "partner" to represent *neged* in the translation of this verse, as long as "helper" is retained, it will continue to lend support to the idea of man's superiority. I used to work construction and was a carpenter's helper, and I knew that I was not the equal of the carpenter for whom I worked (this was particularly evident on payday!). Only the NAB has eliminated the idea of woman as helper entirely in its translation.

The word *'ezer* is used more than twenty times in the Hebrew Bible, and in three-fourths of the passages it refers to God's direct assistance to humans. God is an *'ezer* for humans. In Psalm 30:10 comes the cry "O Lord be my helper," and in Psalm 54:4 comes the affirmation "God is my helper." In Psalm 121:1–2 we find "I lift up my eyes to the hills—from where will my help come? My help comes from the Lord, who made heaven and earth." In Deuteronomy 33:26, "There is none like God, O Jeshurun, who rides through the heavens to your help, majestic through the skies." The NJB perhaps best catches the meaning of *'ezer* in this last passage in its translation, "God rides to your rescue." In Exodus 18:4 one of Moses' sons is named Eliezer because "The God of my father was my help, and delivered me from the sword of Pharaoh." In Psalm 10:14, 1 Chronicles 15:26, Genesis 49:25, 1 Samuel 7:12, and Isaiah 41:10,13,14 God is the one who is doing the helping. In these passages God is the *'ezer*, the one who is independent and who is the strong one who comes to the aid of those in need. No one would want to argue in any of these passages that God as helper is the subordinate one in the relationship between God and humans. Yet when the same word is used about Eve, all the translations except the NAB retain some sense of woman as a subordinate helper.[9] Imagine the possibilities for the roles of women and men if *'ezer* were translated as "rescuer," as the one who saves man from the loneliness of an existence apart from someone like him to be in relationship with. Women who work in the home and around their children all day might understand the need for someone like them, someone at their level, to relate to after all day spent with the kids.

The second part of the Hebrew phrase here is *k^eneg^edo*, which has been represented in the above translations by "suitable," "comparable," or "partner." The meaning of this phrase according to the Hebrew lexicon is "a help corresponding to him," that is, "equal and adequate to himself." All the translations except the NAB have retained in some sense the KJV "help meet" despite the translations of *k^eneg^edo* as "companion" or "partner," which ought to mitigate against the concept of woman as one who serves only in a secondary and supportive role as man's helper. If, however, one looks at the evidence from the Hebrew lexicon for the semantic range of *'ezer* as it appears in this phrase, it is difficult to explain the secondary role implied in "help meet" or "helper."

This continues to be so despite the numerous commentaries that argue that the sense of "help meet" as commonly understood is not what is meant here in this passage. Gerhard von Rad argues that in this passage God states that solitude "is not good; man is created for sociability . . . the word $k^e neg^e do$ ('fit for him') contains the notion of similarity as well as supplementation; but one may not here personify *'ezer* ('helper') and translate it 'helpmeet' with reference to the later creation of the woman."[10] And Claus Westermann, in his excellent and exhaustive commentary on Genesis, suggests that the meaning here of *'ezer* can be seen in Ecclesiastes 4:10, which warns, "Woe to one who is alone and falls and does not have another to help." Westermann states, "The man is created by God in such a way that he needs the help of a partner; hence mutual help is an essential part of human existence."[11] Indeed, such understandings of *'ezer* made it necessary for at least one commentator to remind his readers that women are not superior to men: "Some have therefore thought that God made women *superior* to men. But this is not so. Men and women are equal partners."[12]

The movement from needing to argue that this text does not cast women as inferior to having to argue that it does not indicate their superiority is quite a step, and one made possible by a closer look at the possible meanings of the words in the Hebrew text.

Mashal in Genesis 3:16

Here, with italics added, is the text of Genesis 3:11–19 in the NRSV.

> [11]He said, "Who told you that you were naked? Have you eaten from the tree of which I commanded you not to eat?"[12]The man said, "The woman whom you gave to be with me, she gave me fruit from the tree, and I ate." [13]Then the Lord God said to the woman, "What is this that you have done?" The woman said, "The serpent tricked me, and I ate."[14]The Lord God said to the serpent, "Because you have done this, cursed are you among all animals and among all wild creatures; upon your belly you shall go, and dust you shall eat all the days of your life. [15]I will put enmity between you and the woman, and between your offspring and hers; he will strike your head, and you will strike his heel." [16]To the woman he said, "I will greatly increase your pangs in childbearing; in pain you shall bring forth children, yet your desire shall be for your husband, and *he shall rule over you*." [17]And to the man

he said, "Because you have listened to the voice of your wife, and have eaten of the tree about which I commanded you, 'You shall not eat of it,' cursed is the ground because of you; in toil you shall eat of it all the days of your life; [18]thorns and thistles it shall bring forth for you; and you shall eat the plants of the field. [19]By the sweat of your face you shall eat bread until you return to the ground, for out of it you were taken; you are dust, and to dust you shall return."

In Genesis 3:16 the Hebrew has *w^ehu' yim^eshal bakh,* which the KJV, NRSV, NASV, and NIV translate variously as "he will/shall rule over you." The NAB has "he shall be your master," the NLT has "he will be your master," and the NJB has "he will dominate you." Indeed, these are translations whose words have resulted in great pain for women in the church through the ages. Even worse is the possibility that it was unnecessary pain that might not had to have been endured if, again, one considers all the possibilities in the Hebrew lexicon for the word *mashal.*

The Hebrew lexicon lists two roots for the word *mashal.* Stem I means "represent, be like," while stem II means to "rule, have dominion over, reign." Dr. Thomas McDaniel, in class lectures at Eastern Baptist Theological Seminary as early as the 1970s, argued that perhaps the translators of the Bibles then extant should have considered the possibility that the author of Genesis might have intended the meaning of "to be like, similar" and not "to rule over." Since then there have been many new translations of the Bible in English, but none of them included this possibility in either the text of Genesis 3:16 or even in the footnotes.[13]

It is true that in the Hebrew lexicon *mashal* is not attested in the *Qal* (the basic dictionary form of the verb) for stem I ("to be like") but is attested in stem II. This is true, however, only if one argues that here in Genesis 3:16 the meaning "rule over" of stem II was intended by the original author and not the "to be like" of stem I. It is only the opinion of the lexicographers, followed by the translators and the commentators, that the *Qal* imperfect *yim^eshal* here in 3:16 is from stem II and not stem I. Since the form would be exactly the same in either stem, there is no way to distinguish between them except for context, and it is entirely possible that either stem would fit in the context of this passage. A clear, plausible, meaningful translation of the Hebrew text might read,

> To the woman he said, "I will greatly increase your pangs in childbearing; in pain you shall bring forth children, yet your desire shall be for your husband, and he shall be like you."

The possible point of this text, then, is that the act that nine months later results in pain (and perhaps more than just the pangs of childbirth, but also the subsequent pain that children often can cause in their relationships with both mother and father, a pain shared by both) is still desirable and "your husband shall be like you," that is, "shall desire you." The superiority of men over women is then not supported or required by the Hebrew text *wᵉhu' yimᵉshal bakh*.

This possibility, while not yet reflected in any translations of the Bible, has at least begun to be considered in discussions of Genesis 3:16. "Whereas traditionally the woman's submission to her husband was accepted as an ordinance of creation that was corrupted by the fall and can only be restored through the Christian gospel, new voices propose that Eve's submission was an altogether new state resulting from sin."[14] And among a number of possible interpretations of Genesis 3:16, Davidson mentions the argument for reading *mashal* as stem I, meaning "like," which would affirm original equality.[15] The most complete and convincing argument in print is that of J. J. Schmitt, who argues that this verse speaks of a mutual sexual desire of men and women even though this makes even more certain the pain of childbirth and "child-rearing."[16] Matthews does, however, dismiss the possibility of *mashal* as "like" in Genesis 3:16 on the basis that the "linguistic support is not strong,"[17] although he does not really critically evaluate the arguments for "to be like" as the sense of the Hebrew text here.

H. G. Stigers sees this verse in a broader sense of a woman's economic or emotional reliance on her husband, and her desire to be submissive to the man is in no way resisted by him.[18] In an attempt to take some of the "hurt" for women out of this verse, M. Stitzinger argues that the submission called for becomes a punishment only when the husband takes advantage of his position and abuses her.[19]

Perhaps the following words from Ralph Elliott best indicate the futility of such an approach.

> For women the punishment was painful and difficult childbirth, for sin disrupts the harmony of God's creation. In addition, her desire was to be toward her husband, who would exercise tyrannical domination over her (3:16). It is important to note again that these things are perversions of what was intended. When a right relationship with God is established, as much of this as possible should be removed and rectified.[20]

Elliott goes on to indicate the nature of what it is that he means should be removed and rectified: "Today the validity of such understanding is being championed by the medical profession, which recognizes some possibilities for 'painless' childbirth when the mother is emotionally mature."[21] Where is there any thought for the pain of having been denied the opportunity of equality in faith and ministry, and how can emotional maturity in faith come while subordination continues to be the reality for many women in the church?

The Painful Consequences of These Translations and Understandings of ʿEzer and Mashal

Paul, in my view, in several passages (most notably 1 Corinthians 11; 14; Ephesians 5; 1 Timothy 2) argues for the superiority of men over women, and despite the efforts of many recent commentators to "rescue" Paul and insist that this is not what he meant, other commentators and much of the Christian church from Paul onwards have so understood Paul. The wish by many recent commentators to remove Paul, in the above passages, from among those supporting the subordination of women in the church is admirable, and their arguments are creative, scholarly, and well intentioned, but on the whole are unconvincing in light of the uniformity in agreement of the translations of the Greek text of 1 Corinthians 11.[22] Paul does not quote Genesis 2 or 3 in any of these passages, but it is interesting to observe that in 1 Corinthians 11, Paul's choice of the Genesis 2 account of creation allows him to argue for a hierarchy in the church. Here is the text of 1 Corinthians 11:3–9 in the NRSV.

> [3]But I want you to understand that Christ is the head of every man, and the husband is the head of his wife, and God is the head of Christ. [4]Any man who prays or prophesies with something on his head disgraces his head, [5]but any woman who prays or prophesies with her head unveiled disgraces her head—it is one and the same thing as having her head shaved. [6]For if a woman will not veil herself, then she should cut off her hair; but if it is disgraceful for a woman to have her hair cut off or to be shaved, she should wear a veil. [7]For a man ought not to have his head veiled, since he is the image and reflection of God; but woman is the reflection of man. [8]Indeed, man was not made from woman, but woman from man. [9]Neither was man created for the sake of woman, but woman for the sake of man.

By selecting the second account of creation and ignoring Genesis 1:25–27, Paul can argue that woman is not made in the image of God (this seems clear from all the English translations) and is therefore the "reflection of man." Traditionally, most commentators have understood Paul's argument here as just that and as support for the subordination of women.

> [T]here is a conscious parallelism between subordination to the man in the home . . . and subordination in the congregation to the "teachers." That this is also Paul's understanding is clear from the similar argument in I Corinthians 11:3–16 where the subordination of women is manifested in the service of worship by the fact that she, who is not God's image but only that of man, must wear a veil.[23]

The comments of James Moffatt (who during his lifetime was an enormously popular commentator on the Scriptures in conservative churches) are representative of much of the understanding of 1 Corinthians 11 by many like-minded Christians.

> The sweeping statement at the start goes further than Paul needed to go, but he wished to find a sanction for his ruling in the original hierarchy of the universe laid down in Genesis. . . . Man as the Lord of creation would be violating the law of his position under God, as God's direct likeness and representative, if he suggested, even in dress, any inferiority. At worship, as elsewhere, his headship must be preserved. A male being exhibits on earth the divine authority and dominion, as he was directly created by God; he has supremacy over the female who in turn represents the supremacy of man. . . . the veil that covers her head is a sign or symbol of this subordinate position, to be worn out of reverential respect.[24]

In a similar vein, Frederik Grosheide sees Paul as arguing that only a man is both in the image and glory of God.

> If Paul had used the word "image" only, the woman might point to Genesis 1:27 and say that she too was in the image of God. But Paul writes: *image and glory of God* and adds in vs. 7c of the woman that she is *the glory of the man*. . . . *Glory* does not here have the meaning of the full divine majesty. . . . That is why Paul can write that a man, who is in the image of God, reveals how beautiful a being God could create, which makes him the crown of creation, the glory of God. A woman, on the other hand, reveals how beautiful a being God could create from a man.[25]

Some wish to blame it on the Jewish heritage of Paul, and so George Tavard, in discussing 1 Corinthians 11:2–7, writes, "This is patently a very rabbinic passage. Paul has not yet emancipated himself (and how could he have done so?) from the thought patterns of his Jewish-Pharisaic training."[26] Arguably, that thought pattern included a concept of the subordination of women that the traditional translations[27] and understanding of *ezer* as helper made possible.

William Barclay also wants to blame Paul's words here on his Jewish heritage. "We must remember the status of women in Jewish eyes. Under the Jewish law woman was vastly inferior to man. She had been created out of Adam's rib (Genesis 2:22–23) and she had been created to be the helpmeet of man, for man's sake (Genesis 2:18)." A few lines later he adds, "It is the unfortunate truth that in Jewish law a woman was a thing and was part of the property of her husband. . . . In Jewish law and custom it was unthinkable that women should claim any kind of equality with men."[28]

Craig Keener argues that here Paul "says because woman was taken from man, she reflects man's image, and therefore ought to cover that image in worship lest it detract observers from attention to God's image," and Paul is addressing only the issue of women in church and not equality, that "it is not that Paul is unaware that woman and man together make up God's image. It is impossible that he had not read the explicit statement to that effect in Genesis 1:27."[29] But commentators and translators and church leaders throughout the ages have read that explicit statement in Genesis 1:27, and it has not stopped them from arguing that Genesis 2 indicates that only men are made in the image of God and that therefore women are subordinate to men in the church. "Because man is a reflexion of the divine glory, while woman is only a reflexion of that reflexion, 'therefore the woman is morally bound to have the mark of his authority upon her head. . . .' There is no real doubt as to the meaning, which is clear from the context."[30]

Gerda Lerner alludes to another solution for absolving Paul from holding to the superiority of men over women.

> Modern biblical scholarship has reached near-consensus in the judgement that most of the comments pertaining to women attributed to Paul were not in fact written or spoken by Paul but were the product of post-apostolic writers who ascribed the texts to him for greater authority. . . . Knowledge of the erroneous ascription was, of course,

not available to women until the present day, so that for nearly 2000 years the misogynist Paulinist tradition, which has dominated biblical interpretation, was regarded as apostolic.[31]

Much that has been written about Genesis 2 and 3 and the meanings of *'ezer* and *mashal* seems almost ridiculous, and perhaps would be comical were it not for the use made of the traditional translations and understandings of these words to subject women to a position of inferiority in the Christian church. And whether or not Paul wrote the words in 1 Corinthians 11 (and other passages like it), or intended those words to support any hierarchy with man at the top, or was influenced by the understanding of *'ezer* as "helper" or *mashal* as "rule over" and thus intended to argue for the subordination of women, certainly many others have understood these words to establish the dominance of men as ordained by God both in Genesis and in Paul's writing, and "until the present day" women continue to be hurt by the tradition of woman as a helper to be ruled over by her husband.

Despite the excellent modern scholarship that has proposed alternatives for the translations of *'ezer* and *mashal*, no recent translations of the Bible have included these understandings. Instead, Southern Baptists vote to deny women the opportunity to pastor churches; the pope, the head of the largest segment of Christianity in the world, reaffirms repeatedly, in no uncertain terms, that women cannot be priests; and organizations such as the Promise Keepers continue to grow and attract increasing support. All quote Genesis 2 and 3 as part of the foundation for justifying their positions and practices. The translations of these words and the focus on the second creation account, which had allowed the argument that only men are made in the image of God, have contributed to the perpetuation of the subordination of women in much of the Christian church and continue to cause a great deal of pain and hurt in the lives of many Christian women.

Questions for Further Reflection and Discussion

1. That the Hebrew words *'ezer* and *mashal* have several levels of meaning has been known for over a century. Given this, why do you think the church has fixated on the meaning that supports women's subordination to the neglect of the other possibilities?

2. Based on this discussion, how important do you think it is that pastors be able to study the Bible in its original languages?

3. How is your understanding of the Bible as divine revelation affected by the fact that biblical words can be translated in more than one way?

4. Do organizations like the Promise Keepers and the Southern Baptist Convention have the authority to keep women in subordinate roles within the family and church? If so, what is the source of that authority?

Endnotes

1. I am indebted to Dr. Thomas McDaniel, my friend and my teacher at Eastern Baptist Theological Seminary, who knew the ability of words to hurt but who persevered so that we, his students, might learn to use them in other ways. I first heard of other possible translations for these words in the Hebrew text of Genesis 2 and 3 in classes with him and thus am indebted to him on many levels for this essay.

2. I am amazed at the reaction to the heading "Another Account of the Creation" in the New Revised Standard Version by students in my classes in Intellectual Heritage, in church groups, and in the introductory classes in Old Testament at Eastern Baptist Theological Seminary. The idea that there are two creation stories has long been accepted by scholars but continues to be a new idea to many outside of the community of biblical scholars. Most often the explanation is that Genesis 2 is just another telling with some different nuances from Genesis 1. This ignores the reality that the two stories cannot be forced into agreement with each other, especially as to when women are created, and this has been too often ignored by too many.

3. Online: http://207.240.176.152/Articles/2000/06/SLA6.asp (italics added).

4. Online: http://www.sbcannualmeeting.org/sbc00/ news.asp?ID=19276114 50&page=.

5. Online: http://www.now.com.

6. F. Brown, S. R. Driver, and C. A. Briggs, *A Hebrew and English Lexicon of the Old Testament* (Boston: Houghton, Mifflin and Company, 1906), 740–41.

7. This is an accurate translation if one understands the King James English sense of "meet." According to Melvin Elliott, "meet" as an adjective means "qualified," "fitting," "suitable," or "appropriate" (*The Language of the King*

James Bible [Garden City, N.Y.: Doubleday, 1967], 116). Frequently the two words have been combined into "helpmeet," which often has been taken to mean "helpmate," which serves only to reinforce the idea of woman as "helper." Here once again the language of the King James Bible is misunderstood, as is so often the case, even with those who have read it all their lives and refuse to consider any other translation.

8. All scripture citations are from the New Revised Standard Version of the Bible unless otherwise noted. Hereafter, the following abbreviations will be used for the various translations:

NRSV—New Revised Standard Version

NIV—New International Version

NASV—New American Standard Version (1995)

KJV—King James Version

NKJV—New King James Version

NAB—New American Bible

NJB—New Jerusalem Bible

NLT—New Living Translation

9. Ironically, in many congregations the word used of God as rescuer or savior appears in the phrase from the traditional hymn "Come, Thou Fount of Every Blessing," where the second verse begins, "Here I raise mine Ebenezer. . . ." This verse is a reference to 1 Samuel 7:12, where "Samuel took a stone . . . and named it Ebenezer; for he said, 'Thus far the Lord has helped us.'"

10. Gerhard von Rad, *Genesis: A Commentary,* trans. John H. Marks, rev. ed. (Philadelphia: Westminster Press, 1972), 82. But this is exactly what Paul does in 1 Corinthians 11.

11. Claus Westermann, *Genesis 1–11: A Commentary,* trans. John J. Scullion (Minneapolis: Augsburg, 1984), 227.

12. John Hargreaves, *A Guide to Genesis* (London: SPCK, 1998), 28.

13. Many translations of the Bible include notes on the translations of various words in their text. Sometimes the notes tell us what other manuscripts have at that point in the text, and other times they indicate other translators' opinions about variant possible translations. To this point, no English translation that I am aware of has even mentioned in a note the possibility of another alternative to "rule over" as the translation of *mashal.*

14. Kenneth A. Matthews, *Genesis 1–11:26* (Nashville: Broadman and Holman, 1995), 248. In my view, there has been little restoration of the idea of

submissiveness in any positive sense by the Christian gospel throughout most of Christianity.

15. R. M. Davidson, "The Theology of Sexuality in the Beginning: Genesis 3," *Andrews University Seminary Studies* 26 (1988): 121–31.

16. "Like Eve Like Adam: *mšl* in Gen 3,16," *Biblica* 72 (1991): 1–22.

17. Matthews, *Genesis 1–11:26*, 250.

18. H. G. Stigers, *A Commentary on Genesis* (Grand Rapids: Zondervan, 1976), 80.

19. M. Stitzinger, "Genesis 1–3 and the Male/Female Role Relationship," *Grace Theological Journal* (1981): 23–44. However, the husband retains the "position" of authority.

20. Ralph Elliott, *The Message of Genesis* (Nashville: Broadman Press, 1961), 49–50. One can almost hear the cries of women, "How long, O Lord?"

21. Ibid., 50.

22. See, for example, Craig Keener, *Paul, Women and Wives* (Peabody, Mass.: Hendrickson, 1992), 19–47; Elisabeth Schüssler Fiorenza, *In Memory of Her* (New York: Crossroad, 1986), 226–30; Katherine Doob Sakenfeld, "Feminist Uses of Biblical Materials," in *Feminist Interpretation of the Bible*, ed. Letty M. Russell (Philadelphia: Westminster Press, 1985), 55; Leonard Swidler, *Biblical Affirmations of Women* (Philadelphia: Westminster Press, 1979), 329–32.

23. Krister Stendahl, *The Bible and the Role of Women* (Philadelphia: Fortress, 1986), 29.

24. James Moffatt, *The First Epistle of Paul to the Corinthians* (New York: Harper and Brothers, 1960), 151–52.

25. Frederik Grosheide, *Commentary on the First Epistle to the Corinthians* (Grand Rapids: Eerdmans, 1953), 255–56.

26. George H. Tavard, *Women in Christian Tradition* (Notre Dame, Ind.: University of Notre Dame Press, 1973), 29.

27. The Septuagint, the first translation of Genesis, has *boēthon*, for which Liddell and Scott give the following meanings: "come to aid, succor, assist, aid." As an adjective it has the sense of "ready or able to help, serviceable," and often in prose with the sense of "assisting, auxiliary, or assistant" (*A Greek-English Lexicon* [Oxford: Oxford University Press, 1977], 320).

28. William Barclay, *The Letters to the Corinthians* (Philadelphia: Westminster Press, 1956), 109. While many would wish to argue with Barclay's

representation of Jewish law in these statements, Barclay was a well-known and popular New Testament expositor, widely read by a large segment of the Christian church. Although he goes on to say that it would be wrong to make a universal application of these words from Paul, he has no doubt what Paul meant by them.

29. Keener, *Paul, Women and Wives*, 37.

30. Archibald Robertson and Alfred Plummer, *A Critical and Exegetical Commentary on the First Epistle of St. Paul to the Corinthians*, 2nd ed. (Edinburgh: T. & T. Clark, 1958), 232.

31. Gerda Lerner, *The Creation of Feminist Consciousness* (New York: Oxford University Press, 1993), 140.

CHAPTER 3

Who Killed Goliath?
History and Legend in Biblical Narrative

ROBERT F. SHEDINGER

There are few biblical images more firmly embedded in our cultural heritage than that of David, the young shepherd boy, slaying Goliath, the Philistine giant, using nothing more than a sling and a stone. In the sports world, when the underdog team upsets the powerhouse team, the image of David killing Goliath is frequently invoked to emphasize the magnitude of the upset. Or in the business world, when the small, upstart company challenges the large, established corporation for market share, the small company is said to be fighting against Goliath. This image is so deeply embedded in our culture, it seems, primarily because everyone loves an underdog, but also because the David and Goliath story is a favorite of our childhood Sunday school classes. How often were we told as children that David overcame all odds to defeat the giant because he had been faithful to God and God was fighting on his side? How often has the message of this story been articulated as supporting the claim that God fights on the side of the one who is faithful?

A more important question, perhaps, might be raised: How often have we actually sat down to read the story of David and Goliath in all its details? Does this narrative as it appears in the Bible really support the lesson so frequently derived from it? Will God rush to our side and defeat our enemies, no matter how implausible the circumstances, if we are just faithful enough? I believe that a close reading of the biblical narrative of David and Goliath calls many of these ideas into question. The narrative is not as neat and tidy as it is usually presented. And when the various critical issues are taken seriously, it leads us, I believe, to see God's revelation in this story in an entirely new light: not as a story about how God fights for us, but as a story about how we appropriate God to give divine legitimacy to our own, all-too-human penchant for seeking violence and revenge against our real or perceived enemies. Let us turn to the text, then, and see what the Bible really has to say about David and Goliath.

The narrative of this widely known biblical battle is, for the most part, found in 1 Samuel 16–17. The story begins in chapter 16:14, where we find King Saul tormented by an evil spirit. In an effort to find relief, Saul orders his attendants to find a musician who can play for him and soothe his troubled spirit. His attendants hear about a young man named David, who is a son of Jesse, and who is highly skilled at playing the lyre. Saul sends a message to Jesse, asking that he allow his son David to come into Saul's royal service as his official court musician. Jesse responds positively, and David, in his role as court musician, becomes an intimate associate of Saul. Whenever Saul is attacked by the evil spirit, David plays his lyre and calms Saul's troubled soul.

At this point, chapter 17 begins with a description of a giant warrior of the Philistines named Goliath of Gath. He is described as being nearly ten feet tall, fully clothed in a suit of bronze armor, and carrying a spear the size of a weaver's beam—a warrior of truly legendary proportions. He taunted the Israelites to come out and fight him, but the Israelites, including King Saul, were understandably terrified and avoided any confrontation. But just as the story is beginning to build to a climax, as we wait with bated breath to see who will have the courage to fight this fearsome warrior, the narrative abruptly changes course at 17:12 with what appears to be an entirely new introduction to the story.

Now we are told that David is the son of an Ephrathite of Bethlehem named Jesse. But, of course, we have already been told this in 16:18, so this new introduction seems an unwarranted interruption to the flow of the story. But the new story unfolds, and we now find David working for his father by tending to his father's sheep and carrying provisions to his brothers, who are fighting against the Philistines on the front line. In the course of making repeated supply runs to the front lines, David sees Goliath and hears his taunts. But at this point we must raise this question: What happened to the David who was working as Saul's official court musician? We find him now working for his father as if he had never left to go play his lyre for Saul, as if, in fact, he had never had any previous contact with the king at all.

Nevertheless, on one of his supply runs to the front, David decides to hang around talking to the men. His older brother Eliab sees this and becomes angry, castigating David for leaving their father's sheep unattended. Then abruptly again, at 17:32, we find David back in the presence of Saul and volunteering to go out and fight against Goliath. Saul, of course, tries to talk him out of it, but David is relentless, and Saul finally agrees to let him go. In a humorous aside, Saul suits David up with Saul's armor, but alas, David is too small and the armor too heavy. He is unable to move with it on. So removing the armor, David elects to face Goliath with nothing more than a sling and a stone.

As the two improbable adversaries come face to face, Goliath taunting David all the way, David reaches into his pouch, pulls out a stone, and slings it at Goliath. The stone strikes the giant squarely in the middle of the forehead, knocking him down. At this point the story becomes rather more muddled. In 17:50 the narrator tells us that David prevailed over the Philistine with a sling and a stone, knocking him down and killing him. Then the narrator, in order to glorify the power of God that was with David, boasts that David did not even need a sword to kill the giant. But in the very next verse we are told that David stood over the fallen warrior, pulled out a sword, killed Goliath with it, and then cut off his head. So did David kill Goliath with nothing more than a sling and a stone, not even needing a sword, as verse 50 boasts? Or did he first knock him down with a stone, at which point he grabbed a sword, killed the fallen Goliath, and cut off his head, as verse 51 relates?

The David and Goliath story, short of being a clear, consistent narrative, is actually a rather confusing account with several significant inconsistencies. But even more confusing is what happens next. Upon witnessing the fight between David and Goliath, Saul is understandably impressed, and he begins to ask his attendants who this young boy is who has done the impossible by slaying the fearsome giant and who is his father. But remember, in the very beginning of the narrative it had already been established that David had a very close relationship to

Saul, and Saul had even sent to David's father to ask permission to have David come into his service. Saul was even the one who earlier had put the armor on David and sent him into battle. Now, in the aftermath of David's improbable victory, Saul is completely ignorant of the identity of this young hero!

If this were not enough to make us question the consistency of the narrative, we must now jump forward to 2 Samuel 21:19. We are now near the end of David's life, and due to his age and failing health, he has nearly been killed in battle. His men command him to retire from active combat and to leave the fighting to them. Then they go out in battle against the Philistines, and we are told in verse 19 that an Israelite from Bethlehem named Elhanan killed Goliath of Gath, "the shaft of whose spear was like a weaver's beam." Because of the way Goliath is described here, using the same exact phrase as occurs earlier, there is no question that this is the same Goliath we met in the earlier narrative. And this leads to the important question: Who killed Goliath? Was it David, who pulled off the improbable victory as a young shepherd boy turned court musician to Saul? Or was it Elhanan, one of David's men, who did it when David was old and had retired from active combat?

This glaring inconsistency between the earlier David and Goliath story and this account of Elhanan's defeat of Goliath is a problem not only for us; it caused a considerable problem for an ancient writer as well. It has been firmly established by biblical scholars that the Old Testament books of First and Second Chronicles are a very late writing, and that they use the books of Samuel and Kings as source material. In some places the writer of Chronicles copies Samuel and Kings verbatim over large sections. But it is also known that one of the purposes of this late writing was to glorify David as the epitome of what an Israelite king should be. For example, one of the most famous stories about David found in the book of 2 Samuel, one that sheds a very negative light on David, involves his affair with Bathsheba and the consequent killing of her husband as a cover up. When we turn to the Chronicles account of David, however, this unflattering story is conspicuous by its absence. The Chronicler consistently cleans up the image of his hero. What will the Chronicler do, then, when he comes upon 2 Samuel 21:19 and finds the notice that it was Elhanan who killed Goliath and not David? The answer comes in 1 Chronicles 20:5. In narrating the same battle between the Philistines and David's forces as was narrated in 2 Samuel

21:19, the Chronicler relates that Elhanan killed Lahmi, Goliath's brother! Faced with an inconsistency in his text, the Chronicler, who, remember, wants to glorify David as the ideal king, introduces a new character into the story, Goliath's brother, in order to save the authenticity of the earlier David and Goliath tradition.[1]

Of course, one might argue that the Chronicler really did know an authentic tradition about Elhanan killing Goliath's brother, and that he really was correcting the text of 2 Samuel 21:19. This is, of course, possible. But then we have an error in 2 Samuel 21:19. So no matter how we look at it, the biblical tradition about the Philistine giant, Goliath, is a disjointed one. Who killed Goliath, David or Elhanan? If it was David, did he do it with a sling and stone or with a sword? Why does Saul not recognize David after the battle when it was Saul who sent David into battle in the first place? Why is there a second introduction of David in the middle of the narrative, just as the story seems to be building to a climax? Any authentically biblical understanding of the David and Goliath tradition must consider these questions. Fortunately, the evidence exists for answering some of these questions, and for gaining insight into how the David and Goliath tradition developed in biblical antiquity. It is this understanding that will lead us to draw a theological lesson from this tradition quite different from the one we have traditionally been taught.

First we must consider some biblical history that, while it may seem off the topic, will be important for our understanding of the development of the David and Goliath narrative. In the year 586 BCE, the Babylonian Empire overran the area of Palestine, destroying everything in its path. This included, of course, Jerusalem and the Jewish temple. The Babylonians took some of the Israelites away to Babylon as exiles, while they left the rest of the population behind to scratch out a living in a desolated land. Because of the difficulty of life, many of the people left this area and settled in other lands. This movement became known as the Jewish Diaspora, a scattering of the Jewish people following the destruction of Jerusalem.

Some of these Jews settled in the city of Alexandria in Egypt, and over time they became a large and thriving Jewish community. Alexandria, however, was a thoroughly Greek city, and this Jewish community gradually lost its ability to speak and understand Hebrew, the language of their Israelite heritage. This, of course, meant that they lost the ability to read and understand their Scriptures, all of which were written in Hebrew or the related language of Aramaic. By the third century BCE, the situation had become so critical that they began to translate their Bible into Greek for use in synagogue worship. They began with the Pentateuch, the first five books of their Bible, and eventually translated their entire Scriptures into Greek. This Greek version of what Christians commonly call the Old Testament became known as the Septuagint.

While the Hebrew Bible continued to be used in the Jewish communities in and around Palestine, the Septuagint became the Bible of Diaspora Jewish communities, including the one into which the apostle Paul was born in the city of Tarsus. When we turn to the New Testament, we find that Paul and most of the other writers make almost exclusive use of the Septuagint when they quote from the Old Testament. The Septuagint became, for all intents and purposes, the Old Testament of all early Christians, a fact that is easy to understand when one realizes that Christianity became very early a predominately Greek-speaking religion.[2] Thus, in the first century CE, the time of Jesus and immediately after, there were at least two versions of the Old Testament in existence: the Hebrew Bible of Palestinian Jews and the Greek Septuagint of Diaspora Jews and early Christians. But what does all this have to do with David and Goliath?

As disturbing as it might seem at first, the truth is that the Septuagint sometimes differs substantially from the Hebrew Old Testament. This difference is greater in some books than in others. For example, the Septuagint version of Jeremiah is one-sixth shorter than the Hebrew version, and the chapters are in a somewhat different order. Since our English Bibles are translated from the Hebrew text, we read the longer version of Jeremiah. But it is startling to realize that since Paul used the Septuagint, he, in the first century, read a very different version of Jeremiah than we read in our contemporary churches.

Now at one time it was thought that the translators of the Septuagint were responsible for all the differences, that they had done a poor job translating the Hebrew text. But then, in 1948, the Dead Sea Scrolls were discovered, and scholars found Hebrew scrolls of the Old Testament from the first centuries BCE and CE that agreed with the text of the Septuagint. It became clear that the Septuagint is a good translation of an alternate Hebrew text, and that in the first century CE more than one Hebrew version of the Old Testament existed. The degree of variation between versions differs from book to book, with the most dramatic degree of variation occurring between versions of Jeremiah. But the text of First Samuel differs significantly between versions as well, and First Samuel just happens to be the book that relates the story of David and Goliath. How might this story in the Septuagint differ from the way it appears in our English Bibles, all of which are based on a much later Hebrew text? And what might those differences mean for how we interpret the David and Goliath narrative?

I noted earlier that in the case of the book of Jeremiah, the Septuagint version is one-sixth shorter than the later Hebrew version. Such is also the case in First Samuel, where the Septuagint preserves a shorter form of the David and Goliath story. In this shorter version, what material is left out? The Septuagint version begins where the traditional version begins, in chapter 16, with David leaving his father and becoming Saul's official musician. The two versions run parallel with only minor differences through 17:11. But then the Septuagint jumps immediately to 17:32, omitting the entire section of verses 12–31.When we look to see what has been left out, we find that this is precisely the section that we noted as seeming to be out of place. It is a new introduction of David that pictures David as working for his father and carrying supplies to the front line where his brothers are fighting the Philistines. This is the section, remember, that seems to interrupt the narrative just as it was building to a climax. There is no such problem in the Septuagint, where the story continues to build. In 17:11 we are told that Saul and all the Israelites were greatly afraid upon hearing the taunts of Goliath. Then in the next verse (17:32) David tells Saul to take heart and volunteers to go out and fight the giant. Thus, there is no interruption in the flow of the narrative.

So David goes out to fight Goliath, and the next significant difference between the Septuagint and the traditional text concerns David's method of killing the giant. The Septuagint preserves 17:49, where David hits Goliath in the forehead with a stone and knocks him down. But the Septuagint omits the next verse, the one that explicitly says that David killed Goliath with a sling and a stone and boasts that he did not need a sword. Thus, when the Septuagint relates 17:51, in which David kills Goliath with a sword and cuts off his head with it, there is no inconsistency in the narrative. In the Septuagint, David merely knocks Goliath down with a sling and stone, but he kills him with a sword.

Finally, the Septuagint omits verses 55–58 of chapter 17, the passage where Saul, after seeing David slay Goliath, is astounded and inquires into David's identity. I remarked earlier that this is problematic because we already know that David worked for Saul and that Saul sent him into battle. How, then, can Saul not know who it is that just defeated the Philistine warrior? No such problem exists in the Septuagint version, where the offending passage is missing.

In brief, then, the Septuagint version of the David and Goliath story is shorter than the traditional version, and the missing passages are exactly those that cause confusion in the traditional version of the narrative. The Septuagint preserves a shorter and more coherent version of the narrative in which David goes to work for Saul, learns about Goliath, volunteers to fight him, and kills him with a sword. Moreover, when the material omitted from the Septuagint is put together as a whole, it constitutes another coherent version of the story, but a different one. In this alternate tradition, David works for his father and has no contact with Saul. As he takes supplies to the front line, he learns about Goliath and volunteers to go out and fight him. Much to the chagrin of his brothers, David squares off with the giant and improbably kills him with nothing more than a sling and a stone. The narrator even boasts that David did not need a sword. Upon seeing this, Saul wonders about the identity of this young man who has done the seemingly impossible. Saul's ignorance of David's identity makes perfect sense in this version because David has had no previous contact with Saul. In making sense out of this evidence, Eugene Ulrich, a professor at the University of Notre Dame and a chief editor of the biblical manuscripts found among the Dead Sea Scrolls, concludes, "The David-Goliath story is a clear example of two different editions of a biblical narrative, both attested in textual witnesses, which in different eras have had long-standing and widespread claim as 'the Bible.'"[3]

What the Septuagint really tells us is that in the ancient world, the story of David and Goliath circulated in two distinctly different versions, and that the traditional text on which our English Bibles are based is a conflation of these two originally independent versions. This is why the traditional version is confusing and inconsistent. In conflating two originally independent versions of the story, conflicting details were brought side by side into the same narrative. When we take this evidence together with the notice in 2 Samuel 21:19 that it was Elhanan rather than David who killed Goliath, it looks as though we are seeing stages of a developing legend about David and the Philistine warrior. This is clear also in one other difference between the Septuagint and the traditional account that I have not yet mentioned. In the Septuagint, Goliath is described as being almost seven feet tall, large, to be sure, but not beyond the bounds of human possibility. But in the traditional version, Goliath has become closer to ten feet tall, a clearly legendary height. As with the man who catches the fish that gets bigger each time he tells the story, we see the marks here of the David and Goliath story being a developing tradition that became embellished and more fantastic over time. I would propose, then, that it was Elhanan, an obscure member of David's army, who killed Goliath in an ordinary battle with the Philistines toward the end of David's life, and that this tradition later was transferred to David's youth in order to celebrate David's status as Israel's great warrior king. First it was the young David killing a seven-foot-tall Goliath with a sword. Later this became a ten-foot-tall Goliath whom David slays with nothing more than a sling and a stone, not even needing a sword. The legend becomes more fantastic over time in order to emphasize that it was God working through David to destroy Israel's enemies. But why would a legend such as this have developed in the first place?

Following the Babylonian destruction of Jerusalem and the Temple in 586 BCE, the Jewish community became powerless vassals in the power politics of the Near East. The Babylonians took a portion of the Jewish community into exile. But the Persian Empire defeated the Babylonians in 536 BCE and returned the Jewish community from exile, encouraging them to rebuild their temple. After a period of Persian rule, Alexander the Great defeated the Persians, and the Jewish community became subject to the Hellenistic empire of Alexander and his successors. Finally, in the middle of the second century BCE, the Jewish community threw off foreign domination in the Maccabean uprising and regained their political autonomy for about a century. But this period of independence came to a crushing end when Rome emerged on the world scene and subjugated the Jewish community once more.

Reeling from the loss of their autonomy once again, the Jewish community began to look back to their earlier history, to a time when they were a world power. They looked back to the reign of King David, for it was during his reign that Israel had achieved its greatest fortunes in terms of military and political power. Under David, the emerging nation of Israel greatly expanded its borders through military conquest, centralized its government in Jerusalem, and began to live in relative peace and stability for the first time in its history. And most of these achievements came about as the result of David's great prowess as a military commander. Since David was a great warrior as an adult, it is natural that this characteristic would be read back into his childhood, much like the legend of George Washington not lying about chopping down the cherry tree gets read back into his childhood to celebrate a characteristic—in this case, honesty—that people experienced about Washington as an adult. In the legend of David and Goliath, the later Jewish community was celebrating the idea that God's power was made manifest in David, even as a young boy, by his remarkable ability to kill off the Israelite's enemies, even in the face of overwhelming odds.

In the context of Roman domination in the first century CE some in the Jewish community began looking for a new David to come and lead the community into battle against Rome and defeat the hated enemy. They called this new David by the title Messiah, the anointed one. Yet, as Christians we believe that this concept of Messiah was embodied in the person of Jesus of Nazareth, for whom there is little or no evidence that he ever led or even considered leading a violent insurrection against Rome. Rather, he talked about loving our enemies and doing good to those who hurt us. In Jesus, we meet the one who tells us that God's power is not made manifest in military prowess or earthly political battles, but in a love so strong that it can transcend the boundaries of human conflict and division.

The David and Goliath story is not a story about how God will destroy our enemies if only we are faithful enough. Jesus was the epitome of faith, but still he succumbed to physical torment at the hands of his enemies. Rather, it is a story about our own human capacity to celebrate violence and to appropriate God to give divine legitimacy to our own longings for revenge on our enemies. In the story of David and Goliath, God holds up to us a mirror in which we see our own humanity, our own private longings for violence and revenge, reflected back to us in all their disturbing details. In this way, the story of David and Goliath as legend, rather than fact, is revelatory. For it reveals to us our own sinful humanity, a revelation that drives us to the cross, where that sinfulness can find redemption.

If the David and Goliath story is a literal, historical account, then we will have to conclude that God does indeed destroy the enemies of the faithful. But this makes the God we worship a God of violence and revenge. If, however, as I have tried to show, the David and Goliath story is a developing legend, it stands not as a revelation of what God will do for us, but a revelation of the way in which we try to remake God in our image as the one who advances our own human agendas. A modern example of what I mean will be helpful here.

A couple of years ago, a young gay man, Matthew Shepherd, was beaten to death in Wyoming because of his homosexuality. During his funeral service, a small crowd of anti-gay protesters gathered outside of the church, some holding signs that read "God hates fags." What were these protesters really telling us? Were they making an objective statement about God's attitude toward homosexuals? Or were they remaking God in their image, using God to give divine legitimacy to their own hatred of homosexuals? If we look to Jesus as the most complete revelation of God available, we see one who showed mercy and compassion specifically toward those groups marginalized by his society. This would suggest that the Wyoming protesters were telling us about their own attitudes and about their willingness to appropriate God to give those attitudes divine legitimacy.

In much the same way, the David and Goliath story is not telling us that God's power is made manifest in violence and revenge. Rather, it is telling us about ourselves and our own capacity to use God to further our own wishes for violence and revenge. Instead of celebrating the manifestation of God's power in the death of Goliath, maybe we should be about the business of identifying our own personal Goliaths, and then following the course of love and forgiveness set forth by Jesus.

Questions for Further Reflection and Discussion

1. What do you think about the idea that God's revelation can be contained in unhistorical legend rather than historical fact? What does it say about our view of God if we claim that God's truth can be mediated only through one genre of literature?

2. What are some of the ways that people and groups in our society appropriate God to give divine legitimacy to their own human desires?

3. What might be some of the implications of the fact that the apostle Paul and other early Christians read a version of our Old Testament that in many ways was quite different from the version we read today?

4. If Jesus had lived in the time of King Saul, what advice do you think he might have given the king regarding the Philistine threat?

Endnotes

1. Second Samuel 21:19 explicitly says that Elhanan was a Bethlehemite, which when written in Hebrew becomes two words written without the vowels, *byt hlḥmy*. In 1 Chronicles 20:5, the Chronicler omits this detail about Elhanan being a Bethlehemite and instead takes the second part of this Hebrew phrase from Samuel, *lḥmy*, and turns it into the name of Goliath's brother, Lahmi. Thus, the Chronicler appears to save the earlier tradition about David killing Goliath by using material already in his source to create the name of a new character, Goliath's brother.

2. I use the term "Old Testament" only for convenience here. The term is anachronistic relative to Paul because it implies the existence of a New Testament, but the New Testament did not yet exist in the time of Paul or other writers of what we know as New Testament books.

3. Eugene Ulrich, *The Dead Sea Scrolls and the Origins of the Bible* (Grand Rapids: Eerdmans, 1999), 37.

CHAPTER 4

An Ancient Formula for a Church/Community in Mourning

Insights into the Grief Process

DEBORAH J. SPINK

Have you ever read Psalm 137? It was written at a time when the Israelites were mourning the loss of their city, their temple, their homeland, and their way of life. What do you make of the last two verses? Would you say that those verses reflect the will of God, or do they express the desires of a people facing a time of calamity?

Psalm 137

¹ By the rivers of Babylon—
    there we sat down and there we wept
    when we remembered Zion.
² On the willows there
    we hung up our harps.
³ For there our captors
    asked us for songs,
  and our tormentors asked for mirth, saying,
    "Sing us one of the songs of Zion!"

^{4} How could we sing the Lord's song
  in a foreign land?
^{5} If I forget you, O Jerusalem,
  let my right hand wither!
^{6} Let my tongue cling to the roof of my mouth,
  if I do not remember you,
 if I do not set Jerusalem
  above my highest joy.

^{7} Remember, O Lord, against the Edomites
  the day of Jerusalem's fall,
 how they said, "Tear it down! Tear it down!
  Down to its foundations!"
^{8} O daughter Babylon, you devastator!
  Happy shall they be who pay you back
  what you have done to us!
^{9} Happy shall they be who take your little ones
  and dash them against the rock![1]

When I read Psalm 137:9, I do not believe that these words tell us that God wants us to take the little ones of Babylon and "dash them against the rock!" Rather, I believe these words reveal the emotions of the once-proud citizens of Jerusalem as they faced death, destruction, and deportation at the hands of their conquerors, the Babylonians. The more I study the Bible, the more I come to realize that it reveals both the nature of God and the nature of humankind. It is what the biblical text reveals about human nature as it faces a time of calamity that this essay will examine more closely.

In one edition of the NRSV, Psalm 137 is subtitled "Lament over the Destruction of Jerusalem." It is an example of a biblical genre that has come to be known as communal laments. These laments are found largely within the Old Testament books of Lamentations and Psalms.[2] They deal with times during which the community is threatened by a natural disaster, a perceived enemy, or an invading army. Interestingly, communal laments are not a novelty of the biblical texts, but are preceded by a history of laments known as the Mesopotamian communal laments.

As scholars began to study the oral and written forms of the communal laments of Ancient Near Eastern and biblical texts, they analyzed the structure of each lament. As the similarities and differences between those structures emerged, questions arose as to the possibility of the influence of the Ancient Near Eastern texts upon the biblical texts. Scholars began to line up for or against the case for the influence of the Mesopotamian laments on the biblical laments.[3] Paul Wayne Ferris Jr., in his analysis of communal laments in the biblical texts and in texts of the Ancient Near East, notices that all of the laments have three things in common.[4] It does not matter whether the lament is from an Ancient Near Eastern text or from the biblical text; they all contain some form of what Ferris calls the "invocation or direct address," the "complaint or lament proper," and the "appeal for deliverance and restoration."

Each of Ferris's phrases is self-descriptive. The "invocation or direct address" occurs when someone calls on the name of God. The invocation usually occurs at the beginning of the text but can occur within the body of the text.[5] The "complaint or lament proper" usually contains two parts, the description of what actually happened and the description of the physical and mental anguish it has caused.[6] The "appeal for deliverance and restoration" pleads with God for rescue and restitution from the calamity, and at times includes the very human response of an appeal for a curse to be placed upon the cause of the calamity.[7]

If we analyze Psalm 137 using this basic structure of invocation, lament, and appeal, it looks like this: The invocation comes in verse 7 as the psalmist calls upon the Lord at the transition between the lament and the appeal. The complaint or lament occurs in verses 1 through 6 as the psalmist reveals the plight of the people. They are no longer in their beloved homeland surrounding Jerusalem but are being held captive by the rivers of Babylon. There they are weeping over their memories of Zion. The last thing they feel like doing is singing, and yet that is exactly what their captors are taunting them to do. Their captors are tormenting and ridiculing them by asking them to sing them one of the songs of Zion. The appeal comes in the form of a curse as the psalmist asks the Lord to remember the day when Jerusalem fell and the Babylonians were crying in victory, "Tear it down! Tear it down! Down to its foundations!" The psalmist then rejoices over the thought of those who eventually will repay Babylon by dashing the children of the Babylonians against the rock.

Although Ferris's goal was to delineate the forms of the Mesopo-tamian and the biblical communal laments to see if there is a "unified comparative description of the Hebrew genre of communal lament: its form and function,"[8] I believe that Ferris has hit upon a deeper issue here. Besides locating the similarities and differences between the Mesopotamian and Hebrew communal laments, Ferris, by identifying commonalities in both sets of communal laments (i.e., invocation, lament, and appeal), also identifies the "form" that the human response naturally follows in the situation of a communal lament. This means that when calamity strikes a community, the community's human response is not "formless." Part of the community's response may have a clearly identifiable form or pattern to it: invocation, lament, and appeal. Using these Mesopotamian and Hebrew commu-nity lament commonalities, we may be able to hypothesize that when a community laments, three things would be expected to happen: First, the community would call on their God. As a modern-day adage says, "There are no atheists in foxholes," meaning when life gets rough, almost involuntarily we turn to a higher and more powerful Being than ourselves—we call upon the name of God. Second, the commu-nity would describe what has taken place, including the physical and emotional blows that the community has suffered. Finally, the com-munity would appeal to God for help through the calamity, and once the calamity is passed, for help in coping with the aftermath of the calamity and in restoring life to some sort of order.

Walter Brueggemann, in his article, "The Formfulness of Grief," shows the importance of communal laments for the church today.[9] First he looks at the form and function of communal laments and then com-pares them with Elisabeth Kübler-Ross's analysis of what Brueggemann calls the "formfulness" or the regular "form" that human grief and death follow. He defines and then analyzes Kübler-Ross's five-element death/grief process with the form and function of the biblical laments. One of Brueggemann's conclusions about communal laments after his analysis using Kübler-Ross's work is that "This community form is nei-ther descriptive nor prescriptive. It is a form in movement, task ori-ented to rehabilitate members to a life world in which transforming intervention is a live option."[10] I believe that Brueggemann is on the right track. Brueggemann is right that there is movement to rehabilitate members (survivors) into a new life; but I also believe, based on the invocation, lament, and appeal commonalities noted by Ferris, that the communal laments in the Old Testament are both descriptive and prescriptive. They are descriptive of what a community will experience as it experiences a calamity that is causing communal lament, and they may also be prescriptive for what a community might expect when facing a situation of communal lament. Let us put our theory to the test.

An interesting observation that Ferris makes is that "whether dealing with the ultimate destruction of the city or a lesser catastrophe, the laments are primarily vehicles of expression for the survivors."[11] What follows next is a situation of communal lament as it has been recorded and reflected upon by a survivor. It is not the story of a natural disaster, nor is it the story of an invading army capturing the city and its temple; rather, it is the story of two teenage dropouts who kidnapped and murdered neighbors in the Westboro neighborhood in the city of Topeka, Kansas. All the victims were members of the same church community, the First Congregational Church.[12]

On December 3, 1989, Tyrone Baker and Lisa Pfannenstiel went to the upper-middle-class neighborhood of Westboro in the city of Topeka, Kansas, looking for a home to break into. After observing an elderly woman who appeared to be working alone in her kitchen, Tyrone and Lisa broke into the home of seventy-two-year-old Ida Mae Dougherty. As they were robbing the home, Ida Mae came upon them. They asked Ida Mae if she had any money. She told them that they could take anything they wanted. Tyrone then proceeded to tie Ida Mae up with duct tape—first her legs, then her arms, and finally her face in such a way as to purposely smother her to death. Tyrone had decided that since Ida Mae could identify them, he had to "do" her (i.e., kill her). Because cigarette burns were later found on Ida Mae's body, it is believed that Tyrone was not sure if he had actually killed her. Apparently, he used the cigarette burns to see if Ida Mae was really dead. He and Lisa then put Ida Mae in her car, drove her outside of town, and "dumped her." Tyrone and Lisa returned and spent that night in Ida Mae's house, opening the Christmas presents she had wrapped and placed under the tree, to see what was worth stealing.

The next morning Lester Haley, one of Ida Mae's neighbors, noticed that Ida Mae had not picked up her paper. Ida Mae rarely picked up her paper later than 8:00 in the morning. Lester and his wife, Nancy, tried phoning Ida Mae, but there was no answer. They grew concerned, so they phoned another neighbor, B. Horne, to ask if they should go and see if Ida Mae was all right. Since all of them were good friends, they had keys to one another's homes. B., who was preparing lunch for her husband, said she would be over as soon as she got her coat and that they should go into the house and check. By the time B. got to the doorway, Lester had opened Ida Mae's door with his key. Lester and B. entered the home and went inside, calling Ida Mae's name. Nothing looked out of the ordinary downstairs, so they went upstairs. There, through a bedroom door slightly ajar, they could see that the bed was unmade and that something was on the floor. They opened the door and were confronted with Tyrone, standing in a corner, holding a gun with both hands, his arms extended.

Tyrone ordered Luther and B. to lie face down on the beds in the other bedroom. He instructed them to remain there and then left the room. After a while Luther and B. heard someone come into the room and knew it was Lester's wife, Nancy, when they heard her say, "Oh, my God!" Tyrone forced Nancy to lie face down between the beds and left. When he came back again, Tyrone told Lester and B. to stand up and remove their glasses, which they all wore. Tyrone tried to put them all in the trunk of Ida Mae's car, but B. convinced him that they would not fit. So he placed them in the back seat of the car and drove them out of town.

When they arrived at a secluded place in the country, Tyrone got them out of the car. B. offered him the diamond ring on her finger and Lester offered him all the cash in his wallet, but Tyrone refused. B. started praying, "God, you've brought us this far. What do I do now?"[13] After they had walked perhaps two hundred yards downhill and were out of sight of the main roadway, Tyrone ordered them to lie face down on the ground. B., with the gun pointed at her, refused to lie down. She told him that whatever happened, she had to see his face. This seemed to stop him. B. said to him, "You've got the car. Why don't you make a run for it? I can sweeten the pot, if you can figure out a way to get me to my bank. I can get you $1,000.00, and you can take that and go."[14] Lester and Nancy offered money as well. Tyrone eventually stated that he was not sure if he had killed Ida Mae or not. B. continued to push her argument, "Well, if she's not dead, you're not a murderer. Why don't you go check?"[15] Tyrone argued that if he left to go check, they would go to the police. B. assured him that they would stay right there and offered to swear on the Bible if he wanted her to. She added that since she was the chief lay leader of her church, he could trust her word. Tyrone bought it. He got in the car, ostensibly to go see if he had really killed Ida Mae. As soon as Tyrone left, B. helped Lester and Nancy to their feet and told them to find a safe place to hide until she could get help. B. stayed away from the road, running from cover to cover, terrified at every noise. Eventually she managed to flag down a car that finally took her to safety and to get help. Within a matter of days, Tyrone Baker and Lisa Pfannenstiel were apprehended, and the bodies of Lester, Nancy, and Ida Mae were found. Tyrone and Lisa were later convicted for the kidnapping and slaying of Ida Mae Dougherty and Lester and Nancy Haley.

This condensed version of the events of December 3, 1989, is based on the 110-page typed manuscript of the sole survivor of the ordeal, Verne Bennett (B.) Horne. It is a manuscript that B. started but has yet to finish. The manuscript contains the full description of what actually happened and the description of the physical and mental anguish it caused then and since. These descriptions are in essence the complaint or lament of the events of December 3, 1989, and what has happened because of those events.

The manuscript also reveals two recorded invocations: the calling upon God by Nancy in her audible "Oh, my God!" and B. in her inward prayer "God, you've brought us this far. What do I do now?" B.'s prayer also reveals her plea for deliverance and restoration. The desire for restoration is also outlined in a detailed "victim-survivor time line" that B. kept, starting with the events of December 3, 1989, and continuing up to Tyrone Baker's last appeal on August 1, 1999. Within her time line B. records her personal development from victim to survivor and the proactive steps she begins to take toward recovery. On April 14, 1996, B. preached a sermon to her community in mourning, the First Congregational Church. The sermon was entitled, "As We Forgive Our Debtors." B. ended her sermon with these words:

> We who were victims can use what we were, what we endured, and the process itself to become survivors. Hear our prayer,
>
> Lord of such amazing surprises as put a catch
>   in my breath and wings on my heart,
> I praise you
>   for this joy, too great for words, but not for
>   tears and songs and sharing;

for this mercy that blots out my betrayals and
    bids me to begin again,
    to limp on,
    to hop-skip-jump on,
    to mend what is broken in and around me,
    and to forgive the breakers.
for this YES to life and laughter, to love and
    lovers, and to my unwinding self;
for this kingdom unleashed in me and I in it
    forever, and no dead ends
    to growing, to choices, to chances,
    to calls to be just;
    no dead ends to living, to making peace,
    to dreaming dreams, to being glad of heart;
How great you are, how full of grace.
Allelulia! [*sic*][16]

In this lament, B. was trying to help her congregation move from invocation, to lament, to appeal for deliverance and restoration, to expression of confidence and hope, and then to the final vow of praise that is a part of many communal laments. When B. proofread this essay for me, she wrote back, "The timelessness of the Bible and its intimate knowlege [sic] of the human spirit continues to surprise me."[17] Earlier in this essay, I stated my belief that the last two verses of Psalm 137 do not reveal the will of God, but rather, the emotions of the surviving citizens of Jerusalem. The emotions struck a chord with B., who wrote back,

> The emotions include overwhelming rage at having been made impotent, unable to stop what was happening. Along with the rage comes grief over family and friends lost, homes gone, treasured mementos destroyed and a way of life torn asunder, never to be re-created. The isolation and loneliness of soul and the guilt that comes from not having been able to be strong enough to conquer the storm, are all a part of it. Emotions also include the victims' need for revenge, which is almost as strong as the rage! These are such passionate statements and are common to all victims. The psalmist knew whereof he spoke.[18]

This essay is but a sampling of further study that needs to be done in the area of communal laments and their impact for our lives today.

As we watch the tragedies that occur in our world community, it is not surprising to see the need for television stations to play over and over again the details of Princess Diana's car crash, the Kennedy-Bessette plane crash, or the Columbine High School shootings. The community at large needs to hear the lament, the complaint, the description of what actually happened and the impact it has on our lives. As those tragedies unfolded on public television, we heard the pleas for prayers for the well-being of Princess Diana, of the Kennedy-Bessettes, and of the Columbine students, all invoking a name of God and appealing for deliverance and restoration. And finally, when the full story is told, the questions of restoration arise: How could these tragedies have happened? How can we prevent such tragedies from happening again?

Walter Brueggemann begins his article with this sentence: "The lament psalms offer important resources for Christian faith and ministry even though they have been largely purged from the life of the church and its liturgical use."[19] Lester Meyer documents how the laments "are underrepresented in the *Lutheran Book of Worship* and in its lectionary."[20] He goes on to detail how 55 percent of the lament psalms are omitted in the Episcopal lectionary's three-year cycle and 68 percent are omitted from the Roman Catholic lectionary.[21] Claus Westermann, in a section of his book on Lamentations entitled "Devaluation of the Lament," writes, "In the Old Testament lamentation is an intrinsic component of prayer, as is shown in the Psalter with its high percentage of psalms of lamentation. In the Christian church, on the other hand, the lament no longer receives a hearing."[22] And André Resner Jr., writes of his concern that within the life of the church "the legitimate cry of lament is silenced."[23] Invocation, lament, and appeal for deliverance and restoration is an ancient formula that gives us insight into the human response of a community in mourning. It is not something that should be ignored or silenced.

Anyone, pastor or layperson, who is leading a community through a time of lament could use this formula to know that there are certain issues that will need to be addressed in an appropriate manner. (1) Invocation: The need to invoke the name of God. Call upon the presence of the All Powerful to be with you. (2) Lament: Tell the story of what happened. Describe the physical, emotional, and mental anguish that is going on. (3) Appeal: Turn to God for deliverance from whatever is causing the calamity. Ask for God's guidance, as the community must face life after the tragedy has passed. These ancient communal laments give us a powerful insight into the human response that occurs during any situation that causes communal lament. The human response of invocation, lament, and appeal can be anticipated and addressed in such a way as to help guide the community through the grieving process. The communal laments have much to teach us. May God help us learn from these sacred words of our ancestors of the faith.

Questions for Further Reflection and Discussion

1. When a tragedy strikes the community at large, how can using the formula of invocation, lament, and appeal be a part of helping a congregation walk through its grieving process?

2. Is it important to be willing to share the details of the tragedy in a public way? Why or why not?

3. How might the study of the communal lament psalms in the Old Testament help us to better understand the human response to the world around us? (See note 2 for a list of communal laments.)

4. Is there anything a pastor, lay leader, or congregation should be wary of when praying for deliverance and restoration in a situation of communal lament?

5. How else might these communal laments be useful either in the life of the congregation or in our personal lives?

Endnotes

1. All biblical quotations are from the *New Revised Standard Version of the Holy Bible* (New York: American Bible Society, 1989).

2. Although there is disagreement over exactly which of the biblical psalms are communal laments, Paul Wayne Ferris Jr., on page 16 of *The Genre of Communal Lament in the Bible and the Ancient Near East* (Atlanta: Scholars Press, 1992), nicely lists all the psalms that various scholars have identified as communal laments, and he bases his own research on identifying

Psalms 31, 35, 42, 43, 44, 56, 59, 60, 69, 74, 77, 79, 80, 83, 85, 89, 94, 102, 109, 137, 142, and the book of Lamentations as communal laments.

3. For a summation of the arguments, see Ferris, *Genre of Communal Lament,* who argues against the case for Mesopotamian influence, and F. W. Dobbs-Allsopp, *Weep, O Daughter of Zion: A Study of the City-lament Genre in the Hebrew Bible* (Rome: Editrice Pontificio Istituto Biblico, 1993), who believes that there was a Mesopotamian influence on the biblical texts.

4. Ferris, *Genre of Communal Lament,* 46, 92, 100.

5. Ibid., 92.

6. Ibid., 95.

7. Ibid., 97.

8. Ibid., 8.

9. Walter Brueggemann, "The Formfulness of Grief," *Interpretation* 31, no. 3 (1977): 263–75.

10. Ibid., 273.

11. Ferris, *Genre of Communal Lament,* 150.

12. I am indebted for the details of this event to the victims and survivor, who allowed me to interview them in person, on the phone, and through e-mail: Sharon Dougherty, daughter of Ida Mae Dougherty; the Revs. Charles and Rebecca Erb, pastors of the First Congregational Church of Topeka from May of 1987 until May of 1995; Dr. Robert Parman, member of the congregation and present moderator; Judith Neher, member of the congregation and moderator right after the tragedy took place; and the sole survivor of the ordeal, Verne Bennett (B.) Horne (who was serving as the church's moderator at the time the tragedy took place), and her husband, Dr. James Horne.

13. Verne Bennett Horne, typed manuscript of events recorded in 1990, 23.

14. Ibid., 24.

15. Ibid., 24–25.

16. Verne Bennett Horne, "As We Forgive Our Debtors," sermon delivered at the First Congregational Church, Topeka, Kansas, April 14, 1996, 7, as adapted from Ted Loder, "I Praise You for This Resurrection Madness," *Guerrillas Of Grace* (Philadelphia: Innis Free Press, 1984), 123.

17. Personal letter to the author from Verne Bennett Horne, April 14, 2000.

18. Comments by Verne Bennett Horne on a draft of the present essay, April 14, 2000.

19. Brueggemann, "Formfulness of Grief," 263.

20. Lester Meyer, "A Lack of Laments in the Church's Use of the Psalter," *Lutheran Quarterly* 7, no. 1 (spring 1993): 70.

21. Ibid., 71.

22. Claus Westermann, *Lamentations: Issues and Interpretation,* trans. Charles Muenchow (Edinburgh: T. & T. Clark, 1994), 81–82.

23. André Resner Jr., "Lament: Faith's Response to Loss," *Restoration Quarterly* 32, no. 3 (1990): 129.

CHAPTER 5

Heaven–
A Place of Revelation
and Discovery[1]

BENJAMIN G. WRIGHT III

In the world of twentieth-century Western society and culture, the word *heaven* conjures an image of a place where people go after dying to receive rewards for a life lived according to God's precepts. Many Christians and Jews have grown up with the belief that heaven is a paradise where the righteous live forever in bliss, or, in some Christian cases, where the righteous wait out the time between death and Jesus' return. This concept of heaven is not a twentieth-century invention, of course, but neither is it a notion that we find clearly or fully articulated in the Bible. Its roots lie primarily in postbiblical Jewish and Christian literatures.

In addition, heaven is frequently contrasted with "that other place" or "that place down there," namely, hell, the locus of eternal damnation and punishment. So, while the righteous have their destination of rest and bliss, the evil have a corresponding afterworld of punishments and eternal anguish.

Yet, when we examine the sacred texts of the ancient Israelites, those books collected in the Hebrew Bible, the Christian Old Testament, these ideas are all but impossible to find. Heaven in this collection is not some paradisaical garden of eternal life, but simply the place where, ancient Israelites believed, God lived. God was, of course, also thought to live on a mountain (Sinai/Horeb), in a tent (what English translations often render as "the tabernacle"), or in a temple, but God's ultimate place of residence was in heaven. Even the English word *heaven* as distinguished from "sky" creates problems. Our English translations of the Bible are a bit misleading, since in Hebrew and Greek there is no separate word for heaven as distinguished from the sky. A single word is used, *shamayim* in Hebrew, *ouranos* in Greek. In Genesis 1, for example, God creates "the heavens and the earth," and establishes the great lights, the sun and moon, in the heavens. In other places, such as the Psalms, God's throne is said to be in heaven. "I lift my eyes to you whose throne is in heaven," exclaims the psalmist in Psalm 123:1. Psalm 11:4 pictures God as "The LORD's throne is in the heavens." In short, as Psalm 115:16 remarks, "The heavens are the Lord's heavens, but the earth he has given to human beings." God belongs in heaven, and people belong on the earth.

So what did the ancient Israelites think happened to people when they died? In short, after death people went to the place of the dead, Sheol. This place, often translated as "the Pit" (RSV), is one of darkness and death, and is conceptualized as the lowest place in the cosmos in contrast with heaven, the highest place. "If I ascend to heaven, you are there; if I make my bed in Sheol, you are there" (Psalm 139:8). The prophet Amos expresses this contrast similarly: "Though they dig into Sheol, from there shall my hand take them; though they climb up to heaven, from there I will bring them down" (Amos 9:2). It is important to note that even though Sheol is where the dead reside, it is not a place unreachable by God. Both these texts assume God's ability to be in Sheol. What is clear, however, is that whatever euphemism the Hebrew Bible uses for what happens after death, being "gathered unto one's fathers" or going down into Sheol or the Pit, in it one does not go to heaven to claim a reward.

One might trace the genesis of the transformation of heaven from a place where God lives to the place of eternal life and bliss to the Second Temple period[2] and the developing idea of resurrection. Daniel 12:1–3 envisions the fate of those who die in the "time of anguish such as never has occurred since nations first came into existence" as an awakening/resurrection where some will awaken to everlasting life and others to everlasting contempt. The righteous will shine like the stars in the heaven. A growing dualistic view of the cosmos and the notion of a future resurrection prepare the conceptual ground for some Jews to theologize about what happens to those who are waiting for the resurrection or what will happen to them after it. Ideas about future resurrection and recompense, of course, find perhaps their most widespread acceptance in rabbinic Judaism and nascent Christianity, but even the New Testament does not show any developed notion of heaven as the place of eternal reward for the righteous (as we will see).

Even though heaven was not thought about primarily as a destination of the righteous dead for eternal reward, it still was a locale of tremendous mystery and importance. Why? One of the reasons—besides the fact that God lived there—was that heaven was the source of the revelation of God's secrets. Only through direct contact with the divine, usually via an ascent into heaven, could those specially chosen by God learn what only God could reveal. The most characteristic places to find these contacts are in Jewish visionary texts called apocalypses, although heavenly ascents are not unique to them. Not all apocalypses contain journeys to the heavens, however, nor is the content of those revelations uniformly the same. In some cases the seer is not even transported to heaven, but heaven comes to the seer, usually in the form of an angel who mediates the divine revelation. This is the case in a work like the biblical book of Daniel. The content of the Jewish apocalyptic visions from the Second Temple period tends to be of several kinds, most frequently the revelation of the workings of the universe; the unveiling of the fates of the righteous and unrighteous, often including eschatological visions; the interpretation of the meaning of the historical past and the prediction of the future; and sometimes the communication of things specifically said to be unutterable.

In what follows I will look at three examples of early Second Temple Jewish apocalypses and then some New Testament texts that contain revelatory ascents to heaven. By juxtaposing these ancient Jewish apocalypses with the later New Testament passages, we learn that only by setting the New Testament writings in the historical, literary, and theological contexts of the ancient Jewish matrix out of which Christianity arose can we attempt to understand a world and people essentially alien to ours. One of the fundamental challenges of biblical exegesis and preaching in a Christian context is to uncover as well as possible that essentially alien world and set it over against the comforting and familiar biblical world we have constructed for ourselves.

Heaven and the Jewish Apocalypses

THE ENOCH CORPUS

I begin with two of the oldest Jewish apocalypses. In their present forms both are contained in a composite work called *First Enoch*. This work survives in complete form only in the Ethiopic language called Ge'ez, although it was originally written in Aramaic and passed into Ethiopic via a Greek translation. Several sections of the work have survived in Greek, and some Aramaic fragments were discovered near Khirbet Qumran among the so-called Dead Sea Scrolls. *First Enoch* is made up of five distinct Enochic works of varying dates: the Book of the Watchers (chapters 1–36), the Similitudes or Parables (37–71), the Book of the Luminaries (72–82), the Dream Visions of Enoch (83–90), and the Epistle of Enoch (91–108). Of these five, I will examine the Book of the Watchers and the Book of the Luminaries.

The Book of the Watchers

The Book of the Watchers (usually dated sometime before 175 BCE), which like the larger Enoch corpus reveals the use of various source materials and accretions over time, is an elaborate version of the myth of the sons of God told in the Bible in Genesis 6. Although Enoch might not be a prominent biblical character in terms of the amount of time the Bible spends on him, one very important claim is made about him: he does not die. Genesis 5:24 reports that "Enoch walked with God, and he was no more, for God took him." Enoch's imputed righteousness in an age of evil and God's removal of him are almost certainly the inspiration for the choice of Enoch as the seer in this and other Enochic works. After all, when God "took" Enoch, where was he taken? Into heaven.

In the Book of the Watchers, as in Genesis, the sons of God, here called Watchers, notice human women and find them desirable. They leave their heavenly abode and take women as their wives, an action regarded by the tradition as sinful. They impregnate the women, who bear a race of giants. The stories in both Genesis and *First Enoch* result in God's intention to destroy these giants in a flood. *First Enoch*, however, ranges far beyond what the biblical account transmits. The Watchers reveal to human women spells, other magical practices, and the "cutting of roots and herbs." The offspring of the illicit relations between the Watchers and the women create havoc on earth, and subsequently humans cry out to God for the giants' destruction.

At this juncture, the narrative trains its focus on Enoch, whom God commands to go to the Watchers and announce their condemnation. The Watchers react in fear and shame, and they beseech Enoch to intercede with God on their behalf. Enoch has a dream vision in which he is transported through the different levels of the heavens until he stands before the very throne of God. On his way he sees various celestial phenomena, but, although they are described in some detail, they are not the primary revelation. When Enoch reaches God's presence, God informs him that the Watchers' pleas will be denied. Only then do Enoch's heavenly revelations really begin.

Chapter 17 begins with Enoch being taken to a great mountain, where he sees "the places of the luminaries and the chambers of the stars and of the thunder peals." He is then shown a number of the wonders of creation, including the "storehouses of all the winds," the actions of the four winds, and "the cornerstone of the earth." The small section between 17:1 and 18:5 is almost certainly a fragment of some earlier Enochic tradition about the revelation of celestial secrets.

At 18:6, however, the narrative suddenly shifts to another series of revelations. God now grants Enoch a vision of the places of punishment of unrighteous people and angels and places of rest for the righteous. These locales are not in heaven, however, but on earth or at the ends of the earth.

Enoch's heavenly revelations end in chapters 34–36 with another short section in which he is transported to the ends of the earth, where he sees "great and glorious works [of creation] at the ends of the whole earth." These visions primarily reveal "the gates of heaven" out of which come weather phenomena.

Enoch whom "God took" is thus the beneficiary of two kinds of tours, and he experiences two kinds of revelations. He learns the inner workings of God's creation, which are generally hidden from human beings, and he witnesses eschatological realities, namely, the prejudgment fates of those righteous and unrighteous who live in heaven and on earth. Enoch is shown these wonders only by being taken to heaven, and the things that he sees could be revealed only there.

The reasons that the author of the Book of the Watchers utilizes the device of Enoch's heavenly journey involve the conditions of his own time. Enoch's revelation indicates that the evil of the time has heavenly causes; it is more than earthly evil. George Nickelsburg suggests that the events described in chapters 6–11 may have to do with the wars, assassinations, and general chaos incited by the military successors of Alexander the Great, and that chapters 12–16 condemn a corrupt and defiled priesthood, most likely that in Jerusalem.[3] Thus, the authors of these Enochic tales mythologize the evils known to them, and they read them back into the paradigmatic stories of evil from primordial times.

The Book of the Luminaries

Dating to the third or perhaps even the late fourth century BCE, the so-called Book of the Luminaries is perhaps the most ancient Jewish apocalypse. Its textual transmission is clouded in obscurity, but it is clear that the version extant in Ethiopic in *1 Enoch* 72–82, and so also in the Greek from which it was translated, is not the original version. Aramaic fragments found among the Dead Sea Scrolls contain material not contained in the Ethiopic version and demonstrate that the original Aramaic document was much more extensive than the Ge'ez translation preserved by the Ethiopic Christian church. In addition, none of the Aramaic pieces from Qumran were copied on the same scroll as the other Enochic works, and thus the Qumran community probably had several Enoch works that were not yet combined under one cover.

The Book of the Luminaries recounts a tour of the heavens given to Enoch by the angel Uriel. The first verses of this work adequately summarize its content: "The Book on the Motion of the Luminaries of the Heaven, how each one of them stands in relation to their number, to their powers and their times, of their names, and their origins, and their months. . . . And [Uriel] showed to me their whole description as they are, and for the years of the world to eternity, until the creation will be made anew to last forever" (72:1).[4] In the subsequent revelation Uriel shows and explains to Enoch in excruciating detail the relative workings of the sun, moon and stars, the gates out of which each comes and into which each goes, and the duration of the time periods governed by each body.

The end of the Book of the Luminaries makes clear why its author chose the heavenly journey for the framework of the book.

> Blessed are all the righteous ones, blessed are those who walk in the
> path of righteousness and do not err like the sinners, in counting
> their days in which the sun travels in the sky, entering in and coming
> out from the doors for thirty days, together with the leaders of the

thousands of the orders of the stars, together with the four (days) that are added in order to separate the intervals (of the year, i.e.) the four intervals, the parts of the year, which lead them and with which they make their entry on four days. There are people who err concerning them by not counting them in the reckoning of the year, for such people err and do not know them correctly, although they belong to the computus of the year and are truly recorded forever. (82:4–6)[5]

The knowledge revealed to Enoch in the Book of the Luminaries indicates that in this period Jews were engaged in a controversy over how the calendar should be set. The temple authorities reckoned the Jewish year on the basis of a lunar calendar of twelve months of twenty-eight days each. When the calendar was out of sync with the sun by a full month, a thirteenth month was intercalated to bring the cycle of the sun and the lunar calendar back together. The angel Uriel reveals to Enoch that the luminaries work not on a lunar schedule of twenty-eight-day months or on a different version of a solar calendar that did not intercalate extra days, but on a 364-day calendar with twelve months of thirty days and four intercalated days. In short, *First Enoch* claims divine sanction for a Jewish calendar different from that of most other Jews and from the Torah (Bible). By claiming divine revelation for such a calendar, the Book of the Luminaries intends to supercede not only the lunar calendar but the very authority on which it is based.

The implications are obviously quite dramatic. Different communities would observe Jewish festivals and holy days on different days if they were set according to varying calendars. This could have disastrous consequences for temple service, for ascertaining days and times on which a Jew could not work, and so forth. In the Book of the Luminaries, and other Jewish works of this period such as *Jubilees* or section A of 4QMMT (an important legal text from Qumran), we see a battle taking place in the Judaism of the third to the second century BCE over fundamental issues of how to reckon the calendar. The Book of the Luminaries must have been one of the big guns of the proponents of the solar calendar.

THE TESTAMENT OF LEVI

Before discussing the traditions about the heavenly ascent of Levi, one of the sons of Jacob, I must address the complicated textual problems connected with them. In its most complete version, Levi's journey to heaven is contained in the *Testament of Levi,* one of a series of pseude-pigraphic[6] deathbed speeches by the sons of Jacob known as the *Testament of the Twelve Patriarchs.* The *Testaments* as we now have them are probably a Christian reworking of Jewish source material, although some scholars believe them to be Christian compositions.

For the *Testament of Levi,* scholars are fortunate enough to have fragments of an Aramaic Levi Document that was a source of the work now found in Greek in the *Testaments of the Twelve Patriarchs.* Several fragments of it were identified among medieval manuscripts discovered in a synagogue *geniza,* or storeroom, in Cairo, Egypt, while other pieces of Aramaic Levi came to light among the scrolls found at the Dead Sea. In addition, one Greek manuscript from the monastery at Mount Athos, designated MS e, contains several longer insertions in the Greek *Testament of Levi* that apparently were translated from the Aramaic Levi Document. Although it served as a source for the Greek Testament, it is clear that Aramaic Levi was not identical to it but was longer than the Greek and had a different order of events. The Greek *Testament of Levi* most likely dates from a period later than the other texts examined here, but its major source, the Aramaic Levi Document, probably dates from the end of the third century or the beginning of the second century BCE. Aramaic Levi, then, is practically contemporary with the two Enochic works discussed above, and, while the relationship between the Greek *Testament* and the Aramaic Levi Document is complex and the subject of much scholarly debate, we can use the two together as indicators of the content of the work.

Levi experiences two heavenly journeys, neither of which is extant in the Aramaic Levi fragments. In *Testament of Levi* 2, Levi has insight into the corruption and sin of human beings. In his grief at the state of humankind, he prays to God that he might be saved. The Greek Testament only notes that he prayed, while Aramaic Levi and Greek MS e preserve the text of the prayer. After he concludes his prayer, Levi sleeps and has a vision of the heavens opened, from whence an angel calls him to enter. In this first vision, Levi sees seven heavens. The angel explains the function of each heavenly realm. The lower three have to do with God's judgment of the unrighteous, while the upper four contain God's throne room and various angels and authorities. Levi is here told to understand the eschatological judgment of human beings, and he receives the message that God has separated him out for the priesthood.

In this vision Levi sees heavenly realities, not in order to understand their inner workings as in the revelation to Enoch, but to learn how they function in God's eschatological plans.

Levi's second vision takes place in heaven, where he sees the temple of God. In this temple, before God's own presence, Levi is invested as the first of the priests of Israel. This vision is followed up in chapter 8 with the angelic investiture of Levi with the priestly garments. The image of Levi in these passages as the perfect priest contrasts with his predictions that later his descendants would make themselves impure through illegitimate marriages and, as a result, defile the temple in Jerusalem. Thus, for the author of this work, God not only establishes Levi as the first and paradigmatic priest but also reveals to him that his progeny, who are the contemporaries of the author, would fail to live up to his example. The heavenly journey of Levi is the vehicle for a rehearsal of history up to the time of the author, complete with diagnosis of the causes of the present situation.

THE BOOK OF BEN SIRA (SIRACH)

At roughly the same time that the communities and authors who produced the Book of the Luminaries, the Book of the Watchers, and the Aramaic Levi Document were speculating about the content of their heroes' heavenly journeys, a scribe named Joshua ben Eleazar ben Sira, usually called simply ben Sira, was teaching prospective scribes in Jerusalem. The book that survived to bear his name was fully extant only in a Greek translation made from Hebrew by the author's grandson.[7] Then in the 1890s the same Cairo Geniza discovery that revealed the Aramaic Levi fragments was also found to contain fragments of six different manuscript copies of ben Sira's book in Hebrew. In the 1940s a small fragment was found in Cave 2 at Qumran and a large section, containing parts of chapters 39–44, was unearthed by Yigael Yadin in the excavations at Masada conducted from 1963 to 1965.

Ben Sira's notions of heaven and Sheol are consistent with those in the Hebrew Bible that I described above. The dead go to Sheol/Hades, where they live a shade life separated from the living. Sirach 41:3–4 succinctly express ben Sira's thoughts about Sheol: "Do not fear death's decree for you; remember those who went before you and those who will come after. This is the Lord's decree for all flesh; why then should you reject the will of the Most High? Whether life lasts for ten years or a hundred or a thousand, there are no questions asked in Sheol [*Hades* in NRSV]."

Ben Sira almost never speaks of God's dwelling place, and consequently the uses of the Greek and Hebrew terms for heaven refer primarily to the sky. In several places heaven is contrasted to the earth (see, for example, 1:3; 16:18). In chapter 43, where he praises the works of God's creation, the heaven/sky is the location of the heavenly luminaries and the stars. In two places ben Sira may be referring to heaven as God's dwelling place. In 46:17, speaking of the prophet Samuel, he remarks that God "thundered from heaven and made his voice heard with a mighty sound." Whether or not this is meant to describe thunder, ben Sira sees the sound as coming from God. Ben Sira's report of Hezekiah's reign rehearses the Assyrian siege of Jerusalem. When the Jerusalemites prayed to God, "The Holy One quickly heard from heaven, and delivered them through Isaiah" (48:20).

For ben Sira, whose conceptions of heaven and Sheol were entirely conventional, heavenly ascents were fundamentally dangerous, potentially misleading, and they should not be pursued. He tried to implant in the minds of his students the notion that heavenly journeys like those taken by Enoch and Levi should not be trusted and that one should be wary of the kind of knowledge provided by such adventures. Three passages are appropriate for our discussion: Sirach 3:21–24, which concerns the revelation of secrets of the universe; 34:1–8, which expresses worry about the mechanisms by which this knowledge is revealed; and 43:6–8, which is a polemic against the solar calendar. My discussion of these texts comprises only a small part of a larger argument in which I conclude that ben Sira is aware of groups like those that produced Aramaic Levi and the Enoch books and their criticisms of what might be called Jerusalem Judaism.[8] He knows their claims that the priests in Jerusalem are corrupt and that they defile the temple; he knows that these groups appeal to heavenly journeys as the authority for a calendar different from the one he uses; and he uses the occasion of his teaching to warn his students about such ideas.

Sirach 3:21–24

Sirach 3:21–24 is part of a larger poetic section on humility and wisdom. These three verses constitute a short statement against the kind of teaching that we saw above in the apocalypses. We have to take a quick look at ben Sira's language, because the passage does not come right out and say against whom it is directed.

> ²¹ What is too marvelous for you, do not investigate,
>   and what is too difficult/evil for you, do not research.
> ²² On what is authorized, give attention,
>   but you have no business with secret things.
> ²³ And into what is beyond you, do not meddle,
>   for that which is too great has been shown to you.
> ²⁴ For many are the thoughts of the sons of men,
>   evil and erring imaginations.

In verse 21 the NRSV translation, based on the Greek, enjoins one not to "seek what is too difficult." The Hebrew is a bit different. It says, "What is too wonderful/marvelous for you do not investigate." The term translated "wonderful" occurs elsewhere in ben Sira to refer to the works of God's creation. In 11:4 this adjective modifies the phrase "works of the Lord," a phrase usually meaning the works of creation. The same term is applied to the wondrous creatures of the sea in 43:25, and a variant form of the same word describes God's works in 42:17.

Ben Sira uses a second important term meaning "secret things" in the very next verse. These "secret things" most likely refer to what will happen in the future. Sirach 42:19 claims that it is "secret things" that God is able to reveal. In fact, God has already revealed "secret things" to the prophet Isaiah (Sirach 48:25). This passage positions this term in parallel with the revelation of "past and the future." Of course, it is entirely appropriate that God would reveal these matters to someone like Isaiah, whose prophecies are part of ben Sira's holy Scripture, but it is more problematic to claim revelatory insight if one does not possess, at least in ben Sira's eyes, the stature of an Isaiah.

Ben Sira urges his students in verse 23 not to meddle in things that are beyond them, because they have been shown enough already. The use of the word "shown" is particularly poignant here, since ben Sira is most likely referring to the Torah (which is "shown," as it were, to all Jews), but those who claim the authority of heavenly journeys are also "shown" heavenly realities.

In short, in 3:21–24 ben Sira encourages his students to study the Torah, which contains all the revelation they need. It is not necessary, indeed not profitable, to go chasing after revelation of the secrets of the universe or the way in which the future will unfold. All the revelation one needs is contained in the tradition that has been handed down.

Sirach 43:6–8

Whereas 3:21–24 outlines in a general way the kind of knowledge that ben Sira found problematic, his comments about the moon in 43:6–8 show more particularly his opposition to one of the primary features of the revealed knowledge of the apocalypses that we have discussed, the use of a solar calendar.

> 6 It is the moon that marks the changing seasons,
> governing the times, their lasting sign.
> 7 By it we know the sacred seasons and pilgrimage feasts,
> a light that wanes in its course.
> 8 The new moon, like its name, renews itself;
> how wondrous it is when it changes!
> An army signal for the cloud vessels on high,
> it paves the firmament with its brilliance.

Two aspects of this passage demonstrate ben Sira's rejection of a calendar based on the movement of the sun. First, a comparison of 43:6–8 with 43:1–5, which features the sun, is illuminating. Those first five verses of chapter 43 treat the sun in an interesting, if prosaic, manner— it is hot! The better part of two verses says simply that. After it rises, it parches the earth; it is hotter than a furnace; it scorches mountains. In verse 5 ben Sira emphasizes God's control over its course. The three verses devoted to the moon, however, all emphasize its function in marking seasons, times, festivals, and the new month (twenty-eight-day cycles, not the thirty-day cycles of the solar months). Second, ben Sira, who clearly knows the Pentateuch, diminishes the role of the sun from that outlined in Genesis 1:14. There, when creating the sun and the moon, God says, "Let there be lights in the dome of the sky to separate the day from the night; and let them be for signs and for seasons and for days and for years." Where Genesis ascribes at least a cooperative role for the sun in calendrical reckoning, ben Sira eliminates it.

Of course, the Book of the Luminaries depicts Enoch's revelation of the workings of the sun and moon as the basis for use of a solar calendar. Aramaic Levi, even though the calendar is not one of the things revealed to Levi, uses a solar calendar in the description of the birth dates of Levi's sons. Ben Sira rejects a solar calendar, in particular, just as he rejected attempts to learn the secrets of the universe in general.

Sirach 34:1–8

In this passage ben Sira disparages reliance on dreams as a means of revelation. Dreams and omens are for him simply the projection of the desires of the dreamer onto the supernatural world. Or, as he puts it, "What is seen in dreams is a reflection that mirrors the vision of the onlooker" (34:3). Dreams deceive those who trust in them, but those who follow the law fulfill it without deceptions.

¹ Empty and false are the hopes of the senseless,
   and fools are sent winging by dreams.
² Like one grasping at shadows or chasing the wind
   is whoever puts his trust in dreams.
³ What is seen in dreams is a reflection
   that mirrors the vision of the onlooker.
⁴ Can the clean produce the unclean?
   Can the liar ever speak the truth?
⁵ Divination, omens, and dreams are unreal;
   what you already expect, the mind depicts.
⁶ Unless it be a vision specially sent from the Most High,
   fix not your heart on it.
⁷ For dreams have led many astray,
   and those who base their hopes on them have perished.
⁸ Without deceit the law is fulfilled,
   and well-rounded wisdom is the discourse of the faithful.

Although ancient distrust of dreams and visions is not unique to ben Sira, this passage should be considered in light of the texts we have already seen. When read in this way, it is hard not to think that ben Sira is in some way addressing the types of heavenly journeys we saw in *First Enoch* and Aramaic Levi. In each of these works the heavenly journey is initiated through a dream vision. Enoch's ascents to the heavenly throne room are specifically noted to happen while he was dreaming, as is Levi's vision of the seven heavens and his subsequent priestly investiture.

What is interesting in passing, however, is that ben Sira does not want to nullify the possibility of revelation through dreams altogether. In verse 6 he says that only dreams sent "by intervention of the Most High" (NRSV) should be regarded. Unfortunately, he does not say how one would tell a divinely inspired dream from one that is simply self-initiated. It may be that in this verse ben Sira is implicitly granting the legitimacy of those dreams and visions attributed to people in the Torah. After all, how could he speak against the dreams of so famous a dreamer as Joseph?

Heavenly Revelation and the New Testament

Although Christians regard the New Testament as sacred Scripture and thus qualitatively different from other literature, those who wrote the books contained in the Christian Scriptures were human beings who lived in particular times and places and who were influenced by the worlds in which they moved. Some of these New Testament writers also obtained special knowledge and insight by means of heavenly ascents. For them, heaven was the place where special insight and revelation originated. Two of these writers, Paul and John of Patmos, are especially relevant.

PAUL

Besides the Gospel writers, perhaps no New Testament personality figured more prominently in the development of early Christianity than Paul. Yet, when we consider Paul's own career, we find that he had his share of people who disagreed with what he preached. His letters are replete with defenses of his gospel and attacks on those who would disregard it. When he is pushed to the wall in defense of his preaching, he appeals to the specially revealed character of his message. Perhaps his appeal to the revelatory nature of his gospel is even part of what people objected to in the first place. Not everyone, as we saw above with ben Sira, accepted the legitimacy of such claims. Two passages describe Paul's revelatory experiences.

In 2 Corinthians 12 Paul defends himself against people who deny his right to call himself an apostle. One of their criticisms is that he has no letters of recommendation on which to rely. Paul, as a result of the criticism, takes up the issue of boasting and defends himself on the basis of his suffering for Christ. But if that were not enough, he says further,

> It is necessary to boast; nothing is to be gained by it, but I will go on to
> visions and revelations of the Lord. I know of a person in Christ who

fourteen years ago was caught up to the third heaven—whether in the body or out of the body I do not know; God knows. And I know that such a person—whether in the body or out of the body I do not know; God knows—was caught up into Paradise and heard things that are not to be told, that no mortal is permitted to repeat. On behalf of such a one I will boast, but on my own behalf I will not boast, except of my weaknesses. (2:12:1–5)

Clearly, this unnamed person is Paul himself, who can speak of such a cataclysmic experience only in the third person. He will, however, boast on that person's behalf. This ascent, Paul intimates, is beyond anything his opponents have experienced, and it constitutes a crucial argument for his right to call himself a true apostle.

We find the second passage in Paul's letter to the churches in Galatia. In this letter Paul replies to those missionaries of the Jesus movement who claim that gentiles who follow Jesus must observe the Jewish law. He states quite succinctly in 1:11–12, "For I want you to know, brothers and sisters, that the gospel that was proclaimed by me is not of human origin; for I did not receive it from a human source, nor was I taught it, but I received it through a revelation of Jesus Christ." The basis of Paul's gospel, and hence his defense, is divine revelation, not the tradition of human beings. In this case, like the preceding one, Paul has received revelation from heaven that could not be gotten through human transmission and that provides the foundation for and content of his preaching.

JOHN OF PATMOS

However we perceive the message of the New Testament Apocalypse (the book of Revelation), its seer understood himself to have gotten special knowledge of eschatological realities. In this respect he stands directly in the line of earlier Jewish seers like the figure of Enoch in *First Enoch* and that of Levi in Aramaic Levi. The Apocalypse is introduced in chapters 1–3 by a series of letters to seven churches. John's heavenly revelations begin in 4:1–2: "After this I looked, and there in heaven a door stood open! And the first voice, which I had heard speaking to me like a trumpet, said, 'Come up here, and I will show you what must take place after this.' At once I was in the spirit, and there in heaven stood a throne, with one seated on the throne!" John, over the next 17 chapters, narrates the vision of "what must take place" that he saw in the spirit in heaven. Clearly, only John of Patmos, whom God specially chose and brought into heaven, was eligible to receive this bizarre and terrifying vision of the eschatological future.

Conclusion

The "biblical" view of heaven, then, does not center primarily on a place where the righteous go. The responsibility for such a notion must belong to later Christian writers who took the few brief hints in that direction found in the Hebrew Scriptures (their Old Testament) and the emerging New Testament and developed them over time into the concept that dominates most modern views of the place.

What we have seen here suggests that for the biblical writers heaven was the place of God's abode, and God would transport some special human beings to this heavenly realm so that they might learn divine secrets. Stories of such heavenly visits where revelation has taken place were not out of the ordinary in ancient Judaism and Christianity, and many people apparently accepted them as laying legitimate claim to authentic and true knowledge of the mysteries of God. Yes, there were those, like ben Sira and probably Paul's opponents, who perceived danger in these journeys. For his part, ben Sira disparaged the visions of his antagonists and the message for which they claimed visionary authority, but he certainly did not cast doubt on such visions in general, since biblical figures reported having them. For Paul and his interlocutors, those who may have challenged the divine revelation of the apostle to the gentiles in favor of human transmission ended up on the losing side.

Heavenly journeys and visions and a world that for the most part accepted them are truly foreign to us, who most likely cannot even conceive of them occurring today. Imagine if a neighbor were to announce that she had just experienced such a journey where God communicated to her "what must take place after this." We might immediately consider the need for psychotherapeutic drugs.

The claims to revelatory experience of Paul and John of Patmos highlight an important point: what they experienced was acceptable, perhaps even normal, for them and their world, but very abnormal, and probably not acceptable, for us. We can approach Paul's and John's appeals to their experiences as authenticating their messages only from the context of the religious world in which they lived, a world where

God was thought to provide special knowledge and insight to those who ascended into heaven to hear and/or see it. Paul and John of Patmos were the religious descendants of a long line of visionaries. We, two millennia later, can appreciate fully the claims and content of these two New Testament writers and others like them only when we recognize and understand their visionary ancestors.[9]

Questions for Further Reflection and Discussion

1. How does the idea that heaven is the place of God's abode and a place of revelation affect our understanding of other New Testament uses of the term "heaven," such as "kingdom of heaven," a phrase found often on the lips of Matthew's Jesus? (See, for example, Matthew 13:24,31,33.)

2. We saw that some people, like ben Sira, were suspicious of claims to knowledge through ascent to heaven. He also warned to accept only dreams sent from God. Yet even today some people claim to have received knowledge straight from God. Do you think that God still communicates in such ways? If so, how could we tell which, if any, of these claims are legitimate?

3. Can you think of other biblical ideas (e.g., women's roles in society and the family) that would be better elucidated if you knew more about their ancient historical, literary, or theological contexts?

4. How does it affect your thinking about Christian faith and doctrine to realize that rather than being unambiguously and clearly articulated in the Bible, certain ideas that we think of as being biblical were shaped and developed primarily by subsequent Christian tradition?

Endnotes

1. This essay is a revised and expanded form of a lecture, "Heaven as a Place of Revelation," delivered in the Frederic C. Wood Jr. Mini-Lecture Series, Vassar College, May 1, 1995. I am pleased to offer this essay in honor of Drs. Glenn Koch and Tom McDaniel, two men who started me out on the path of scholarship. I am proud to call them teachers, colleagues, and friends.

2. This period is often incorrectly called the intertestamental period. In fact, quite a few Jewish works in this period were composed before the latest

book in the Old Testament, Daniel, and other works were composed in the period of early Christianity. The dates usually given for this period span from the rebuilding of the temple after the Babylonian Exile, that is, the latter part of the sixth or the early fifth century BCE, to the end of the first century CE, following the destruction of Herod's temple by the Romans in 70.

3. George W. E. Nickelsburg, "Enoch, Levi and Peter: Recipients of Revelation in Upper Galilee," *Journal of Biblical Literature* 100, no. 4 (1981): 575–600.

4. The translation is from Matthew Black, *The Book of Enoch or 1 Enoch* (Leiden: Brill, 1985), 389.

5. Ibid., 411–12.

6. The term "pseudepigraphic" refers to a number of Jewish works whose authors are purported to be ancient biblical figures.

7. Ben Sira's book, The Wisdom of Jesus ben Sira, does not appear in the Protestant canon of the Bible. It is included in the Roman Catholic Bible as part of the deuterocanonical Scriptures, a collection also known as the Apocrypha.

8. See Benjamin G. Wright III, "Fear the Lord and Honor the Priest: Ben Sira as Defender of the Jerusalem Priesthood," in *The Book of Ben Sira in Modern Research*, ed. P. C. Beentjes (Berlin: Walter de Gruyter, 1997), 189–222.

9. The following books provide excellent further reading for the nonspecialist. For English translations of *First Enoch* and *Testaments of the Twelve Patriarchs*, which are not in the Jewish or Christian Bibles, see James H. Charlesworth, *The Old Testament Pseudepigrapha*, 2 vols. (Garden City, N.Y.: Doubleday, 1983, 1985), or H. F. D. Sparks, *The Apocryphal Old Testament* (Oxford: Clarendon, 1984). For Aramaic Levi, see H. W. Hollander and M. de Jonge, *The Testaments of the Twelve Patriarchs: A Commentary* (Leiden: Brill, 1985), appendix III. For general reading on Judaism in the Second Temple period and apocalyptic and pseudepigraphic literature generally, see Lester L. Grabbe, *An Introduction to First Century Judaism* (Edinburgh: T. & T. Clark, 1996); John J. Collins, *The Apocalyptic Imagination* (New York: Crossroad, 1984); James C. VanderKam and William Adler, eds., *The Jewish Apocalyptic Heritage in Early Christianity* (Assen: Van Gorcum; Minneapolis: Fortress Press, 1996); Michael E. Stone and Theodore Bergren, eds., *Biblical Figures outside the Bible* (Harrisburg, Pa.: Trinity Press International, 1998); Mitchell G. Reddish, ed., *Apocalyptic Literature: A Reader* (Nashville: Abingdon, 1990).

CHAPTER 6

Honor and Shame in First Corinthians

Paul's Conflict with the Pivotal Values of Mediterranean Society

TERENCE C. MOURNET

The last twenty-five years of the twentieth century were marked by a growing hostility between Middle Eastern and Western nations. This ongoing hostility has been centered on several significant events during the last decades of the millennium, and has been made most evident during the extended conflict between NATO and the nation of Iraq. Although political and military alliances are in a large part responsible for this great tension, there exists a more fundamental and perhaps more deeply ingrained difference between the two sides than might initially be apparent. Apart from governmental policy and political differences, the major distinction between Eastern and Western people is of an ideological and sociological nature. As human beings it is in our nature to expect other people to think and act as we do. When people do not meet our expectations, conflict and tension arise. One could continue this line of thought and argue that all forms of hatred, racism, and ethnic conflicts have their roots in the inability of one or both groups of people to understand each other. This is exactly the case between Western and Eastern cultures—our mutual animosity toward one another often results from our inability or, at times, our unwillingness to understand each other.

What we will observe from this study is that there is a wide cultural gap between Western and Middle Eastern society. Understanding the extent of this cultural gap is vital because the contemporary Middle Eastern societies that we as Westerners find so difficult to understand are in fact the direct cultural descendants of Palestinian society of the time of Jesus. Therefore, by better understanding how Middle Eastern and Western individuals think and interact with their respective peers, we can more clearly envisage the social and cultural setting within which the apostle Paul wrote his first letter to the church at Corinth. This process will enable us to understand more fully the significance of Paul's letter and its importance for the church of today.

Eastern and Western societies are fundamentally different in terms of the relationship between an individual and the greater community. Generally, Eastern individuals are far more concerned with their relationship to and with their community than their Western counterparts are. For example, an Eastern family unit typically consists of the extended family, often including three or more generations living together. These family units in turn exist within a larger community of interrelated families, thereby forming a large, interconnected network that forms the context within which all interpersonal communication takes place. Subsequently, Eastern individuals derive their identity and sense of self-worth from their relationship to and with this greater communal network. In this context, the opinions and decisions of the community have an extremely powerful impact on the individual. An individual rises or falls based upon the status granted to him or her by the community, which is in turn accepted by the individual. This broad sketch of Eastern Mediterranean society is in contrast to modern Western society, where individual independence, self-assertion, and a desire to be a "unique" individual are almost universally sought-after character traits. If the Eastern individual is represented as a branch of a mighty oak tree, then the Western individual is a leaf on that oak tree, a leaf that in time separates itself from its source and is free to blow in the wind—no longer dependent upon or subject to its original constraints. In sum, Western society is largely composed of extremely individualistic persons who understand themselves primarily as independent individuals and secondarily as participants in a community. Our notions of self-worth and value (particularly outside the Christian church) are often based on individual achievement or work apart from community. This modern concept of individualism as expressed in our contemporary Western world would have been unthinkable for an Eastern person both in Paul's time and ours.

These cultural distinctions manifest themselves in how children are raised and taught their respective "ways of the world." Western society that is committed to individualism will structure itself around principles of law and guilt (right and wrong), while Eastern society that is committed to group-oriented relationships will structure itself around principles of honor and shame. In law-oriented Western society children are told to either participate in or refrain from activity based on whether or not they are abiding by the law. Individual responsibility is the operative principle from this particular perspective. Eastern societies, on the other hand, instruct their children to maintain honor and avoid shame. The operative principle in this case is not that of individual responsibility but personal relationship to the community as a whole. All this leads to the conclusion that the concepts of individual self-worth and importance are radically different in Western and Eastern society.

The study of honor and shame in Eastern society has brought much insight into the culture at the time of Jesus and has subsequently helped to illuminate and bring forth new perspectives on the interpretation of biblical texts. This approach is contained within the New Testament discipline called social-scientific criticism. In this context the term *criticism* does not represent a negative attack upon the New Testament, but rather closely adheres to the dictionary definition of *criticism* and therefore refers to the task of making discriminating judgments and evaluations of the biblical text. This discipline has demonstrated that honor and shame were the pivotal values of the first-century Mediterranean world. No social interaction in Eastern society takes place apart from its relationship with and reference to honor and shame within the context of community.

The fact that honor and shame are pivotal values of Mediterranean society is reflected by the great extent to which they are addressed throughout the New Testament. This sociological principle plays an important role in many New Testament books—Mark, Luke, Romans, and Philippians, to mention but a few. In fact, this principle is so widely observable throughout the New Testament text that we can state with confidence that the articulation of Christian faith as expressed in the

New Testament canon addressed persons from within their honor/shame-structured society.

The questions now are these: Can we observe these principles of honor and shame at work in Paul's first letter to the church at Corinth? And if so, what implications does that have for our interpretation of his letter? To answer these questions, we must analyze Paul's writings in an attempt to understand how Paul was addressing the values of the Corinthian people and their relationship as individuals to the community as a whole. The "new gospel" brought forth and preached by the apostle Paul had great implications for the Christian community at Corinth. As we will see, his purpose was not to address individualistic Western concerns, but to address the concerns of a communal society based upon principles of honor and shame.

Understanding Honor and Shame

The particular honor/shame structure that existed in the first century CE was not a static, rigid system that can be described via a dictionary-type definition. Rather, honor/shame needs to be seen as a model within which all personal and communal relationships operate. Honor can be understood as an individual's self-value coupled with the status of that individual in the eyes of his or her social group. It occurs when someone attempts to achieve a certain level of status in a community and the community acknowledges or confirms that social status. Honor is what determines appropriate interpersonal interaction between superiors and their subordinates; an honorable person would not interact with someone of a much lower social class, and generally a person from the lower classes of society did not have the opportunity to interact with a person of high status and honor. As we will see, these concepts play a most influential role in the social dynamic at work in the church in Corinth.

Most New Testament references to honor (e.g., John 4:44; Acts 28:10; Romans 2:7; 9:21;[1] 12:10; 13:7; 1 Corinthians 12:23–24; 1 Timothy 6:1; 2 Peter 1:17) are used in the context of reverence, or respect as often expressed as an action. The New Testament references to shame (e.g., Mark 8:38; Luke 9:26; Romans 1:16; 5:5;[2] 6:21; 9:33; 1 Corinthians 1:27; 11:4–6) are all based upon the Greek word that is often translated as "disgrace, dishonor, humiliation." Generally, these definitions for shame are not helpful, for they basically define shame as the antonym of honor. In order to better understand shame, we must continue to broaden our scope and fit the definition into a societal model that will help clarify the situation that Paul addresses. We will look at the topic from two different perspectives. The first is to analyze honor and shame as defined by a person's relationship to his or her societal structure. Our model can then be made complete by an analysis of honor and shame in the context of individual interpersonal relationships.

Honor and Shame in Relation to Societal Structure

Boundaries are fundamental to every society. Even today in our "modern" Western society we are expected to function within the boundaries established and, at times, enforced by our society. In fact, if anyone were to live completely outside of these societal boundaries, that person would have a difficult time communicating with others and even run the risk of not being understood by his or her peers. A society establishes these behavioral boundaries to help maintain order and to determine what constitutes a normative existence for its people. Generally, these boundaries are implicit rather than explicit rules and regulations that capture and control the collective conscience of the people. Boundaries vary greatly among different cultures today, as they did in the time of the apostle Paul. Today the cultural divide separating Western and Middle Eastern nations is partly due to the different boundaries established by both cultures. Since all human activity is expected to take place within the boundaries defined by societal norms and cultural expectations, it is understandable that Eastern and Western countries have a difficult time understanding one another both on an individual and a national level.

Our model of honor and shame must operate within and relate to these established boundaries. When an established societal class boundary is broken in the Eastern world, the result is shame. Any attempt to cross social boundaries can result in ridicule, hence shame. The contemporary concepts of individual freedom and personal rights so integral to our self-identity as Westerners do not apply to a person of the first-century Mediterranean world. The motivational principle there is not individual freedom but personal sensitivity to the opinion of others. The fear of shame makes people acutely sensitive to social boundaries. Anybody who ignores the social etiquette or the rules of human interaction will incur shame.

If shame is incurred by crossing or breaking boundaries, then it follows that one of the main objectives of an Eastern individual would be to live his or her life within those boundaries in order to obtain and secure honor. As Westerners we can perhaps catch a glimpse of this concept of honor and shame at work within the social dynamics among a group of adolescents. This concept of peer pressure is one of the last remaining examples of honor and shame within the Western world. Following the crowd, which is looked upon negatively in contemporary North American society (especially by parents of adolescents), was in fact the main objective for the first-century Mediterranean! All of this is in contrast to Eastern society, where to this day there is great pressure to maintain and defend the status quo. Eastern society in the time of Paul was structured around the principles of boundary protection and preservation that would in turn guarantee honor. Specific acts and deeds carried out within the political, religious, and economic boundaries of society would help guarantee a place of honor within one's community.

A focus on the second dimension of our honor/shame model requires a look at individual interpersonal relationships. Honor and shame function on an individual level as well as on the previously mentioned communal or corporate level. An individual can exist passively in a state of honor or shame (e.g., Mark 8:38; Luke 9:26; John 4:44; Hebrews 3:3), or be actively honored or shamed by another individual (e.g., Acts 28:10; Romans 12:10; 1 Corinthians 1:27). Several factors are involved in determining an individual's place in the honor/shame system. Of these, gender, political, economic, and even religious status play an important role. Everyday activities engage one in a constant challenge-and-response situation, wherein a person challenges the honor of others and defends against incurring shame.

Honor was often directly related to the public status of an individual. Only educated men were able to attain public office or to hold positions of power in Paul's day. In contrast with the current situation in the Western world, women did not have a chance to achieve positions of status or respect. Eastern Mediterranean society in the time of Paul did not consider women to be equal with men—newly born females were at times left outside, exposed to the elements to die because they were considered worthless. We have examples of letters written shortly after the birth of Jesus that illustrate the disparity that existed, and to some extent still exists, between men and women. They demonstrate what today is a frightening disregard for the sanctity of life and the commonly but not universally recognized equality between men and women. In this respect, honor was primarily a male matter, available only to men, who were in a position of authority. It is in this type of culture that the women of Paul's day struggled for social identification. Because of the entrenched patriarchal Greco-Roman society that existed, women did not have much opportunity to achieve honor, but rather needed to be content with the prospect of avoiding shame. By avoiding shame, they would bring honor to their husband. In practice this involved a home-centered existence by which women functioned primarily as maintainers and members of the household. Their role was to prevent shame from entering their home and to live a life devoted to their husbands.

Shame could also result from giving honor to someone who was shameful. If someone of honor were to extend courtesy to a shameful person or acknowledge them by actions, then the honorable person would be shamed. Shame also resulted by acknowledging the actions of someone who broke the boundaries set by society. Acknowledging or siding with someone outside of the defined boundaries was equivalent to personally breaking those boundaries. We will see later how this was an important issue for the apostle Paul and the Corinthian church.

Now that we have defined a tentative framework for an honor/ shame-oriented Mediterranean society, we can turn to the text of First Corinthians and see how Paul interacts with these pivotal values. A detailed survey is not possible within the scope of this work, but we will look at several sections with this socio-anthropological approach (chapters 1–2: divisions in the church, human wisdom versus God's wisdom, references to crucifixion; chapter 4: Paul's establishment of his status; chapter 5: sexual immorality; chapter 6: legal proceedings; chapter 9: run the race; chapter 12: one body with many members).

In 1 Corinthians 1 Paul addresses the fundamental problem that he will deal with for the remainder of his letter. The divisions in the church (1:10–17) are in opposition to what Paul feels to be the essence of Christian community. His exhortation is for the church to "be united in the same mind and the same purpose" (1:10). The background behind this scenario becomes clear when we interpret this passage from the perspective of an honor/shame-based society.

The factions mentioned by Paul in chapter 1 are the naturally occurring products of interpersonal relationships in an honor/shame-based society, where honor had a male and public face. The members of the congregation at Corinth were forming divisive groups, each claiming allegiance to a particular individual. It is noteworthy that all the groups were formed around males (1:12—Paul, Apollos, Cephas, Christ), and that many members of the congregation were trying to affiliate themselves with one of the honorable leaders within the church and the Christian community as a whole. This process would have been understood in Paul's world as a natural extension of the struggle for societal status. In fact, public speakers and philosophers engaged in debates or other forms of competition would urge their audiences to decide in favor of one speaker or the other. This process was taking place in Corinth. Congregation members were choosing one leader over another in an attempt to achieve an honorable status within the church. The exception to that in 1 Corinthians 1 would be the group claiming allegiance to Christ. In that particular situation Paul is exhorting the people "belonging to Christ" (1:12) to not add to the divisions by claiming a position of honor via a type of "superior" spirituality within the church.

The power play and struggles that are characterized in this factional struggle are most likely not so much the result of doctrinal differences as they are of various individuals struggling for positions of honor within the community. As mentioned earlier, honor and shame could be granted by mere association with a particular individual in the community. Given this premise, it would be likely that individuals within the Corinthian community would begin forming different groups based upon allegiance to a leader (teacher) in order to achieve honor. As individual leaders began to develop a following, continuing polarization would follow until a well-defined honor/shame structure developed within the community. Paul knew that he needed to address this particular foundational problem quickly and successfully in order to provide the church with a chance for a successful future. All of Paul's concerns in this passage regarding unity and harmony within the Christian community stem from this particular cultural setting that existed in first-century Corinth.

The remainder of 1 Corinthians 1 (verses 18–31) deals with two important items: wisdom and crucifixion. Paul interweaves wisdom and crucifixion themes throughout chapters 1 and 2. Why does Paul use these terms together, and how are they related to one another? By understanding the significance of both terms, we will be able to determine their strong relationship to one another and to observe how Paul develops a theme to which he will return throughout his letter.

Corinth was a port city of the Roman Empire. The extent to which Corinth was exposed to and affected by the predominantly urban culture is evident from archaeological excavations. Archaeology has learned much about ancient Corinth and has been able to ascertain what the city was like in Paul's day. Corinth, like most Roman cities of its time, was filled with pagan worship of the many gods and goddesses of the Greeks and the Romans both. Corinth also was the home of many philosophers and teachers who would practice their craft during the day in the marketplace. These philosophers were learned men in their society, and they would have held positions of honor within the community. Their task was to convey anecdotal wisdom and to promote their particular school of thought. Corinthian congregants would have felt quite comfortable with the association between wisdom and honor, and likewise understood Paul's reference to wisdom in that respect.

Crucifixion is the other item in chapter 1 that needs further discussion. During the last two millennia the crucifixion of Christ has become disjointed from its powerful first-century cultural context. Crucifixion was not, as is often thought by contemporary Christians, a noble or respectable way to die; rather, it was the most shameful and horrible method of execution that existed in the Mediterranean. In Roman and in Jewish society crucifixion was a punishment usually reserved for the lower classes of society, namely, slaves and criminals. The Roman Empire used crucifixion as a deterrent against rebellion or crime, and subsequently, crucifixions were often carried out along frequently traveled public roads in order to make a visible, public statement regarding the consequences of crime or insurrection.

Paul's message to the Corinthians regarding wisdom and crucifixion takes on even more powerful and dramatic significance once it is understood that his recipients equated wisdom with honor, and crucifixion with shame. Paul acknowledges the popular status of wisdom and power in Corinth when he writes, "Jews demand signs and Greeks desire wisdom" (1 Corinthians 1:22). Honor was obtained through signs (demonstrated power) and wisdom. Paul's statement "The message about the cross is foolishness to those who are perishing, but to us who are being saved it is the power of God" (1 Corinthians 1:18) pointed to what would have been the common and expected view of the cross itself and the crucifixion of Christ. New converts in the Corinthian church would have struggled long and hard with the concept that the shameful cross and crucifixion of Christ was the only way that led to their redemption. The shame associated with Christian faith is also reflected in Hebrews 12:2, which speaks of the shame of the cross. The confrontation with this shameful redemption is heightened in 1 Corinthians 1:23-24: "We proclaim Christ crucified, a stumbling block to Jews and foolishness to Gentiles . . . Christ the power of God and the wisdom of God." In the eyes of Paul, Christ's shameful death on the cross is now being elevated to a position of wisdom (honor), and the honorable wisdom of human society is being transformed to foolishness (shame). Paul demanded a reversal of the commonly understood honor/shame system in the Christian community at Corinth.

The last several verses, 1:26–31, summarize Paul's vision for a new community that is over and against the accepted Eastern Mediterranean worldview. "Not many of you were wise by human standards, not many were powerful, not many were of noble birth" (1:26) implies that the congregation at Corinth was comprised of a few wise and powerful (honorable) people among a majority of lower-class people. The lower-class members in the Corinthian church would have been in a constant class struggle against the honorable members of the community. Paul provides encouragement to the lower-class members by associating their foolish (shameful) status with the shameful earthly status of the crucified Christ. By this association Paul can elevate both Christ and the lower-class members into a more honorable position while lowering the honor and status of the few powerful and noble members. The elevation of the weak and despised, "God chose what is low and despised in the world, things that are not, to reduce to nothing things that are" (1:28), along with the lowering of the honorable, allows Paul to envision a community where "no one might boast in the presence of God" (1:29).

Chapter 4 provides insight into Paul's own personal struggle for authority, privilege, and honor within the Corinthian church. Paul is caught in a difficult situation as he addresses the community at

Corinth. As we have seen, Paul devoted the opening chapters of his letter to overturning the honor and shame structures that existed throughout the Roman Empire and in the Corinthian church. Paul's argument was clear and precise. He addressed the disunity in the church as a state incompatible with Christian community and contrary to the gospel itself. Christ's shameful death was presented as honorable in God's sight, and human wisdom as made foolish by God (1 Corinthians 1:20). Therefore, the foundation established in chapters 1–3 places Paul in a paradoxical situation that he must address in chapter 4.

The paradox was between Paul's message and his position within the Christian community. The only way that the Corinthian church would accept Paul's letter of rebuke and exhortation was if the church viewed Paul as a man of honor. If he was not a man of honor, individuals within the church (and ultimately the church community itself) would be shamed by listening to and acknowledging Paul. The beginning section of chapter 4 (verses 1–13) is used as an argument to establish the author's credibility and honor. So the paradox is developed: Paul must establish himself in a position of honor in order to proclaim that honor and shame classifications are no longer valid for individuals in the context of Christian community.

Paul's attempt to establish his position of honor is not exclusive to First Corinthians, but is found in several other books of the New Testament, such as Acts (16:37), Romans (11:1), Second Corinthians (11:22), and Philippians (3:5). Paul's claim has secular (Roman society) and religious (Christian society) aspects, and is derived from both who Paul is and what he has done.

Romans 11:1 accounts for Paul's religiously ascribed honor. His three separate claims to honor are based on who he is: (1) an Israelite, (2) a descendant of Abraham, and (3) a member of the tribe of Benjamin. Roman citizens had more honor and therefore more privileges than noncitizens. Paul claims the honor that results from his status as a male in Roman society. This is evident in his ardent articulation of his status as a Roman citizen: "They have beaten us in public, uncondemned, men who are Roman citizens, and have thrown us into prison; and now are they going to discharge us in secret? Certainly not! Let them come and take us out themselves" (Acts 16:37). Paul refuses to leave prison secretly, but insists on a public removal, indicating that he is demanding the restoration of his status and honor in Roman society.

First Corinthians 4:1–13 contains Paul's defense before the Corinthian community. The typical interpretation of this passage is that Paul is declaring his independence from the Corinthian congregation and asserting his allegiance to "the Lord who judges me" (4:4). In the context of our discussion on honor and shame it is clear that Paul is not simply declaring his independence from the judgment of the community, but in fact is asserting his honor in the Corinthian congregation. The next section of the text, 4:14–21, is a telling one because it helps the reader to understand how 4:1–13 would have been understood by its original recipients. Paul is attempting to lessen the impact or damage of his powerful words from the earlier part of the chapter. Paul, like any good communicator, is able to make a powerful point and then lessen the backlash. He writes, "I am not writing this to make you ashamed, but to admonish you as my beloved children" (4:14). This verse demonstrates that the reader would have felt shamed by the preceding section (4:1–13), in which Paul was elevating himself to a position of honor. When Paul elevated himself to a position of honor, the other challengers to his authority would have been shamed. When the competition for honor is over, there is a winner and a loser. By establishing his honor to captivate and command an audience, Paul realized that he would be shaming members of the congregation, so he felt led to soften the blow to his challengers.

Paul also lessened the emotional impact of his argument by placing his relationship to the Corinthian congregation within the context of a father and son relationship. An honor/shame relationship not based on family structures would lack the element of love that Paul alludes to in 4:14–21. A father and son relationship would have allowed Paul to retain his honor while inserting love into the relationship. Paul refers to Timothy as "my beloved and faithful child in the Lord" (4:17). Since Timothy is loved and faithful (subordinate and recognizing the honor of his father), he is representative of the type of relationship that Paul seeks to have with the Corinthian church. To summarize, the paradox presented by Paul employs traditional honor/shame language to make an argument against the honor/shame structure itself.

The next section of First Corinthians marks the beginning of Paul's address to the specific problems in the Christian community. His concern in chapter 5 is in regard to sexual immorality "of a kind that is not found even among pagans" (5:1). Once again he is not dealing with individual, personal sin as understood in a contemporary Western context, but with sexual immorality within the context of Christian community. In what context does this sexual immorality take place? What relationship does sexual immorality have with the honor/shame values in Corinth? We must now address these questions.

Corinth was a city deeply rooted in Greco-Roman culture and religious practices. In addition to the pagan worship that was prominent in Corinth, individual sexual expression outside the context of marriage was encouraged and widely practiced. This is often illustrated from the fact that Corinth became the symbol of commercial love during the fourth and fifth centuries BCE. During that time writers from Athens coined slang terms derived from the name "Corinth" to depict fornication and sexual immorality. Although this extreme view of Corinthian fornication has probably been unfairly exaggerated, first-century Corinth resembled any typical Roman port city, and therefore was, during Paul's time, a place where improper sexual activity with an emphasis on prostitution existed if not flourished.

Although sexual immorality existed in Corinth, it did not have the effect on an individual's honor or shame that one might expect. As surprising as it might seem, extramarital sex and other forms of nonmarital sex, including various forms of incest, were not considered shameful. In a world where honor mostly wore a male face and existed in the public arena, sexuality was not something that could bring shame upon a male. Sexuality was considered to be a private matter, and prostitutes were considered such low and shameful members of society that men were not in competition with them for positions of honor. The opposite was true for the women of Corinth. A double standard existed between the sexual responsibilities of men and women. While men had the relative freedom to engage in any sexual activity, women were not permitted such liberties. Women were expected to retain their premarital virginity and to remain faithful to their husbands after marriage, but a man could visit a prostitute without losing his honor.

Given a woman's means for avoiding shame and upholding her family honor, it is interesting to note that in 1 Corinthians 5 Paul does not seem to be addressing the woman involved in sexual immorality. This is important, because unlike men, women were indeed responsible for remaining sexually pure and faithful to their husbands. Paul is not judging the women (which would have been expected), but is actually pronouncing judgment on the accepted honor/shame structure with regard to sexual immorality. Paul's desire is to redraw the lines of honor and shame, so that male sexual behavior outside the context of marriage can produce shame. In Romans 1:27 Paul condemns the "shameless acts" of the men in that church. That passage helps illustrate Paul's view on the immoral situation in Corinth. Chapters 5 and 6, in continuance with chapters 1 and 2, propose the reversal of the accepted honor/shame values of Eastern Mediterranean society.

Chapter 6 of First Corinthians deals with the problem of lawsuits within the Christian community. Much like ours today, society in the Roman Empire was litigious, but the motivation behind lawsuits in a place like Corinth was different. In contemporary society, legal action is often pursued as a means of financial gain. In contrast, the same primary motivation is not at work in Paul's Roman-ruled Mediterranean. The Roman legal system could be used as another means of gaining honor or incurring shame. Judgments in a court of law would provide another, more public means, for enacting social stratification. An individual could uphold his or her honor or could cause another individual to be shamed.

Paul is passing harsh judgment on a community that is not competent to try trivial cases on its own (6:2). When Paul proposes that the Corinthian congregation preside over their own cases, he is advocating the removal of the legal process from the public arena. If the legal process is made private, then the opportunity to achieve honor or receive shame in the secular (non-Christian) world is reduced, subsequently lessening the communities' dependence on the pivotal values at work in society as a whole. This is not necessarily Paul's primary objective in this passage, but it must have been an influencing factor in his mind as he formulated his letter.

After advocating the removal of the legal process from the public arena, Paul proposes what he considers to be the most important and fundamental principle regarding legal action. The ideal to be sought is the elimination of the legal process altogether. For Paul, even the notion of lawsuits between believers is evidence of a defeated community. The words of 6:7 are powerful: "In fact, to have lawsuits at all with one another is already a defeat for you. Why not rather be wronged? Why not rather be defrauded?" Paul does not want the people of Corinth to be involved in the process of honoring or shaming one another. It is more important to maintain a unified community than to fight for individual positions of status within the community. Once again there is a strong connection to the earlier passages 1:18–31 and 4:8–13. Societal shame (cross and crucifixion) is what God views as honorable: "justified in the name of the Lord Jesus Christ and in the Spirit of our God" (6:11).

In Greece the Isthmian athletic games that took place in Corinth were second in importance only to the Olympic games. These athletic games brought great attention to Corinth and were a vital component of their society. High honor was bestowed upon the leader (or administrator) of these games, as well as upon the victors of the athletic competitions. All the participants were equals and thus could compete freely for the honorable prize. Therefore, athletic competition was another means of achieving honor or receiving shame. This public occasion required a single winner and many losers. Competitors would challenge one another for the very few positions of honor within the competition. Thus, Paul uses the imagery of the Isthmian games in his conclusion to chapter 9. Verses 24–27 are an obvious reference to the games and the honor that is bestowed upon the winners. Since only one runner will receive the prize, "Run in such a way that you may win it" (9:24). For Paul, running the race in order to win needs to be understood in context with the earlier part of the chapter. In verses 19–24 he is voluntarily giving up his personal freedom and privilege (honor) for the sake of the weaker brother or sister. *Running the race to win is to run in a way that would bring about shame in society, but more importantly, honor in the eyes of God.*

This concept can manifest itself in many ways in our society. Paul does not want the Christian to "run the race" to gain financial security or personal gain. Rather, he wants people to abandon their own personal aspirations and status to support and serve others who are not as fortunate—or who, perhaps, do not enjoy an equal position of status. Paul envisions a situation where one runs the race according to God's rules. This is precisely what Jesus did when he associated with "tax collectors and sinners." In doing so, Jesus alienated himself from "honorable" people and brought shame upon himself. Thus, we frequently encounter the charge leveled against Jesus—"Why does your teacher eat with tax collectors and sinners?" (cf. Matthew 9:11; Mark 2:16; Luke 5:30). In the case of Jesus, "running the race" for God demanded that he associate with people who were considered "untouchable" (read, dishonorable).

This was Jesus' way to achieve the goals ordained and desired by God. In the same way, Paul wants the Corinthians to "run the race" according to God's rules because it is only God—not society or other earthly powers—who can bestow true honor and shame on individuals.

Chapter 12 is the beginning of a section about spiritual gifts (chapters 12–14) and their relationship to the community. In this section Paul addresses the Corinthians and the interpersonal relationships that exist within their congregation. The vertical societal relationships that exist within the group are again the target of Paul's argument. Paul is advocating the destruction of vertical interpersonal relationships that lead to honor and shame. For Paul, these honor/shame-based relationships cause division and conflict among the people, and are therefore incompatible with Christian community.

Within 12:12–26 is a strong expansion of the "body" principle that Paul previously articulated (10:17; 11:29). This passage presents the physical body as analogous to the corporate body as represented by the Christian community. The analogy between human society and the physical body was not a unique creation by Paul, but was commonplace in the ancient world and would have been familiar to the recipients of Paul's letter. The distinguishing aspect of Paul's analogy is his use of the individual parts of the body as being different but equal. Typical ancient use of this body analogy was to convey a notion of subservience to the whole or to encourage the lower members of society to remain in their current state and not rebel against their superiors. Paul reworks the body analogy to present his view of the equality of all members of the Christian community. Once again Paul is advocating the reversal or destruction of the vertical levels of personal relationships (honor and shame) that are so corrosive within the context of Christian community.

Paul becomes more specific regarding the problems of vertical relationships within the church. His reference in 1:26 to the existing disparity between some members ("not many of you were wise by human standards, not many were powerful, not many were of noble birth") resurfaces in 12:23–24. His argument that "the members of the body that seem to be weaker are indispensable" (12:22) is possibly a reference to people in the Corinthian congregation who would have occupied the lower levels of society (women, children, slaves). As Paul continues his body analogy, he shifts into direct use of the term *honor*. The "less honorable" members are to be clothed with "greater honor" (12:23), whereas the "more respectable members do not need this" (12:24). Paul desires to elevate the less honorable (shameful) members to positions of honor. More respectable (honorable) members of the community have already achieved a certain level of status within the church, and subsequently do not need additional honor or recognition. By elevating the lesser members of the body, equality is achieved among all members. The equality resulting from the removal of vertical stratification enables members to "have the same care for one another" (12:25). Removal of dissension and equality will result in the unity of the church.

Conclusion

Although we have not had the opportunity to develop fully Paul's understanding of community and his view of honor and shame, we have come a long way in understanding the central thrust behind his letter. Understanding honor and shame as the pivotal values of Mediterranean society during the first century CE helps us better interpret Paul's first letter to the church of Corinth. Honor and shame played a vital role in an individual's understanding of self and in his or her relationship to the greater community. All the arguments in Paul's letter need to be understood in relationship to the deep, universal longing for honor that existed in Roman Corinth and in the greater ancient Mediterranean.

First Corinthians as a letter dealing with honor and shame is not unique in the ancient world. What makes Paul's letter unique is his understanding of honor and shame in light of the crucifixion, death, and resurrection of Christ. For Paul, the "foolishness" of the cross demands the reversal, even the destruction, of the deeply ingrained values of the Mediterranean. Honor and shame are no longer applicable designations for people within the body of Christ.

As the Christian church enters the third millennium, we are faced with a situation not unlike that addressed so many years ago by the apostle Paul. Paul's letter forces us constantly to reevaluate our relationships with one another from within the context of Christian community and beyond the walls of our own churches to the wider Christian church as a whole. What Paul is proposing is not an easy task to accomplish, for it challenges the very foundational ideological principles of Western society—self-gratification, self-indulgence, and self-promotion. If we are to grapple seriously with Paul's message and its implications for us today, we must ask ourselves several difficult questions. For example, Are we constantly striving to overturn the corrosive effects of social levels and class conflict that all too often negatively impact the mission and purpose of the Christian church? This issue is not only about race and gender distinction but has a much more deeply seated premise: every person is equal in the eyes of God. One could very easily apply Paul's principles to other areas of disparity among Christians. One that immediately comes to mind in our highly commercialized Western society is the problem of economic class distinction and its destructive effects upon the Christian community and its witness to the world.

This social-scientific approach to understanding 1 Corinthians is not exclusive of other approaches. The interpretations and conclusions offered here provide the reader with a glimpse of only one particular dimension of the biblical text. It is my hope that the approach taken in this essay will be a supplement, and that it will provide the reader with a fresh insight from the apostle Paul and a challenge for the future.

Questions for Further Reflection and Discussion

1. Paul's letter addressed specific people in a specific place at a specific time. What implications does that have for our interpretation and application of Paul's letters today? Paul's discussion about the Christian faith always related to the daily struggles of the Corinthian community. What implications does this have for you as a contemporary spokesperson for Jesus Christ? Does your faith story relate to other people's spiritual and emotional needs, or are you simply conveying "cold facts" about God?

2. Throughout 1 Corinthians Paul emphasizes the importance of Christian community. What implications does this have for the extremely individualistic, self-centered Western society in which we live? More specifically, what does this mean for the Christian church of the twenty-first century?

3. Paul demanded a reversal of the commonly understood honor/shame system in the Christian community at Corinth. What equivalent reversal should we seek in our contemporary Christian communities? In what ways does contemporary society influence

your church? Are these influences incompatible with the concept of Christian community? How can you reverse them?

4. Running the race to win (cf. 1 Corinthians 9:24) is to run in a way that would bring about shame in Paul's society, but more importantly, honor in the eyes of God. Paul envisions a situation where we "run the race" according to God's rules, with the ultimate goal of abandoning our own personal aspirations and status to help and serve others. In what ways does the Christian life require you to make a conscious decision to act against popular opinion? In what ways are we simply following society's lead when we should be following God's?

5. Paul advocated the destruction of vertical interpersonal relationships that led to inequality among believers. What are the different levels of relationships within your Christian community? Identify those levels. Are they based on economic status? Race? Gender? Education? Age? What can you do to eliminate them from your personal life and from your Christian community?

Endnotes

1. In Romans 9:21, the NRSV presents an antithesis between the "special" and "ordinary" uses of a lump of clay (NIV—"noble" and "common"). This translation is slightly misleading. In the Greek, the antithesis is between "honorable" and "dishonorable" uses of clay.

2. In Romans 5:5, the NRSV uses the word "disappoint" for the Greek term meaning "ashamed."

CHAPTER 7

Unity in the Midst of Diversity

The Early Church at Rome as Reflected in Romans 16

JULIA PIZZUTO-POMACO

A Forgotten Text

Romans 16 receives a mere mention in most commentaries. It is rarely used as a preaching text on Sunday morning, nor is it often a focal point of scholarly debate. However, it has not gone entirely unnoticed.[1] Romans 16 was admired by John Chrysostom, who called attention to it approximately sixteen hundred years ago. In his homilies on Romans he implies that it is a text that is easily overlooked, and he exhorts his readers not to miss its hidden treasures.[2] We could say the same today, for many who expound on the "great truths" of Romans miss the gems hidden away in chapter 16.

It is appropriate here to note that Romans 16 has not always been accepted as the last chapter of Romans. Numerous scholars have questioned whether Romans 16 was originally intended for a Roman audience.[3] The issue has been extensively debated. It is also difficult to pinpoint where the doxology belongs. It appears in a variety of places, including 14:23, 15:33, and 16:25–27.[4]

Many theories have been offered to explain the complexity of chapter 16, including at one time the belief that it was originally written for

Ephesus.[5] Some scholars still hold to this belief, as is demonstrated by T. W. Manson in the revised edition of *The Romans Debate*. Yet F. F. Bruce and Peter Lampe, in that same work, argue for a Roman audience. Both assert in varying degrees that Romans 16 not only points to a Roman destination but also paints a picture of the people who were a part of the Roman Christian community. Scholarly support for a Roman audience is increasing, and thus it seems safe to assume that Romans 16 provides us a window on the early Roman church.

The People Who Worshiped and Ministered Together at Rome

Other scholars have attempted to reconstruct the audience of the text,[6] but the lens through which we analyze the data will be slightly different. This essay uses a combination of social-scientific interpretation, biblical feminist inquiry, and traditional historical-critical tools to uncover the context and message of this important chapter.

A basic reading of Romans reveals that it was not sent to a homogeneous audience. Both Jewish and gentile Christians appear to coexist in the Roman house churches. The state of the Roman church appears similar to the political climate—tumultuous and changing. Relations between Jews and gentiles were strained, mirroring their relationship to the Roman state.

The Roman emperors appear to have had a running interaction with the Jews and subsequently with the Christians. Tiberius is reported to have abolished foreign cults and forced the Jews (as well as Egyptians) to burn their religious clothes and items.[7] Dio later tells us that Claudius had a conflict with the Jews. He notes that their numbers had been growing, and as a consequence Claudius forbade them to hold meetings but did not force them to leave Rome.[8] Reading in Suetonius, we learn that Claudius later expelled the Jews from Rome altogether. Suetonius notes that this action was prompted by disturbances that the Jews had "constantly" made at the instigation of Chrestus (Chresto).[9] There has been much discussion over whether Chrestus is a misspelling of Christ, with most scholars taking it as such. Debate continues about whether the two incidents reflect the same expulsion or two separate incidents. It seems likely that both events occurred, with one resulting in the other. Perhaps Claudius's frustration had been building for some time before he made the final expulsion. Thus, it was probably the Jews, including Jewish Christians, who were forced to leave Rome sometime around 49 CE. We have confirmation of this activity in Acts 18. In verse 2 we read of Priscilla (Prisca) and Aquila, who had recently left Rome because of this expulsion and were at the time in Corinth, where Paul meets them.

The difficulties that the Jews faced in Rome are of key interest to our text. If we contend that we have two groups of people in the Roman church, Jewish Christians and Roman Christians, then this expulsion had a bearing on the whole dynamic of the Roman church. The Roman church, composed of many house churches,[10] was not one unified body but rather diverse in ethnicity, locality, and theology. Thus, when the Jews were expelled and living outside of Rome for several years until Nero began his reign, the church functioned as a mostly gentile entity. Therefore, much of the later controversy that Paul addresses after the Jews have returned to Rome (Prisca, Aquila, and others) is clearly related to cultural differences and theological interpretations. As we will see when we explore the makeup of the audience, the struggles of the early Roman church were over custom, culture, and difference in interpretation. The edict of Claudius is a key to understanding why these differences were so profound. The controversy between Jews and gentiles is by no means foreign to Paul, but is of a different nature in this text because the two groups had been separated and then rejoined. Yet, in the midst of all of this friction a clear call for unity runs throughout the letter.

As we have seen, the environment surrounding the Roman Christians was one of impending danger and doom. Persecution may not have been right at hand, but clearly the tensions were mounting.

We now look to the letter written by Paul and sent to the "beloved" in Rome sometime after the Jews began to return to Rome. It was not written to one church of Rome but to the many house churches that existed in this diverse city. A reading of the text seems to indicate that there are at least four natural breaks in the greetings that suggest the addressing of four or more house churches.[11] It is to this audience we now turn our attention.

Audience/Readers

Let us begin by drawing a picture of the people to whom this letter is addressed. The readers in 1:6–7 are described as "called," and it is said that they "belong" to Jesus Christ. They are referred to as "God's beloved in Rome" and "saints." We learn in 1:8 that their faith was proclaimed throughout the *kosmos* (known world). Paul had not been to see them before, yet in 1:9 he prays for them, and in 1:11 we learn that he longs to visit them. They appear to be people of faith worshiping in churches that Paul himself had not founded, yet with whom he had a connection and for whom he had affection. In 16:19 we are reminded that they have been obedient and that this report has reached "all." The Roman believers were a known entity in the early Christian world, known for their obedience and perhaps for their faith.

By 2:5 it becomes clear that some of the addressees had hard and unrepentant hearts. Paul tells them that they will experience God's wrath. Thus, we can assume that some may not have been Christians or may not have been walking faithfully in the Christian life.

Chapter 8 begins to address those who are Christians. The Spirit of God is said to dwell in them. In 8:14 they are reminded that if they are led by the Spirit, they are children of God. They are adopted into the family and do not have to fear (8:15). The Spirit confirms that they are children of God and have an intimate relationship with the Father (8:15–16). They are also called heirs of God and joint heirs with Christ, possessing the privileges of firstborn sons and an inheritance of eternal life. Some of the terms used here might reflect evidence of relationship ties with unrelated kin, which might be described as "fictive kinship."[12] In referring to each other in familial language, they move their relationships into a deeper level of interdependency. The believers at Rome were children of God and thus part of God's family, implying that they were also in relationship with one another as children of God. There is no distinction made between male or female, slave or free, Jew or Greek. All people, regardless of gender, class, or ethnicity are acknowledged as part of God's family.

A Brief Introduction to the Believers of Chapter 16

A variety of women and men are greeted in chapter 16: twenty-six people, two households, two additional groups of believers, and one *ekklēsia* (church) are greeted. Seven women are greeted and commended by name.[13] An additional two are mentioned in relation to male kin. Seventeen men are named and greeted.

Prisca and Aquila are the first two Christians we meet. They had a church that met in their home. They risked their lives for Paul. They were his companions, referred to in other letters.[14] Much has been made of this missionary couple. Prisca's name appears first in this passage, as it does in a few other New Testament citations.[15] In the ancient world a woman was a man's subordinate, and she was bound to male kin throughout her life. It would have been unusual for a woman to assume a leading or equal role. To write Prisca's name first turns the order upside down. Paul does not seem to make any distinction because she is a woman, for together they are called coworkers and comrades.

Epaenetus was known as the first convert in Asia. He is among their group. Mary is another who is singled out and said to be a hard worker. Andronicus and Junia are identified as relatives or kin of Paul, as is Herodion. Do these people, along with Aquila, who is identified in Acts as a Jew, and possibly Prisca, represent the Jewish population? While we do seem to have a Jewish group, clearly there are people of other ethnic backgrounds found throughout chapter 16. Several names are identified as Greek and others as Jewish. Lampe has found through his extensive research that some of those listed were Jews and others gentiles. He also discovered that they were not all "free" people. According to Lampe, probability suggests that two-thirds of the names listed have some kind of slave affiliation.[16]

Andronicus and Junia are said to have been in prison with Paul and that they are (present tense) prominent among the apostles. They are identified in the text as having been in Christ before Paul. Possibly they were a husband and wife team, as they were paired together in a way similar to Prisca and Aquila. The issue of Junia's gender is key. There has been much debate over whether the name Junia is masculine or feminine, and many biblical scholars now confirm it to be feminine.[17] Ancient commentators, including John Chrysostom,[18] understood Junia to be a woman and an apostle. It was not until medieval times that her gender began to be hotly disputed.[19] In fact, in the second revised edition of the *Textual Commentary of the Greek New Testament* Bruce Metzger comments on the dispute his committee had over whether the name represented male or female, saying that some members could not accept the idea of a female apostle. He points out that the "A" decision in the fourth edition of the United Bible Society's Greek New Testament was in favor of Junia(s) over Julia, the other possible variant of the text.

The "A" decision does not reflect consensus on the gender of the apostle.[20] A variety of contemporary English translations still assert the male contracted name Junias (for Junianus), which was not attested during this time period in the ancient world. Yet the KJV, the NKJV, and the NRSV do understand the apostle to be female.

Ampliatus is called Paul's beloved in the Lord, and Stachys beloved. Urbanus is called a coworker in Christ, and Apelles is said to be approved in Christ. The family of Aristobulus is mentioned, so perhaps Aristobulus himself was not a Christian. The same might apply to Narcissus and his family. Tryphena and Tryphosa were considered workers in the Lord. Persis is called beloved and is singled out for her hard work.

Rufus is called "chosen," and his mother had been a mother to Paul as well. Perhaps she was a wealthy patron of Paul or simply a warm supporter for whom Paul felt a "motherly" affection. Two other groups of people are greeted separately, indicating that perhaps they formed separate house churches. At the conclusion of this section the believers are told that "all" the churches of Christ greet them.

If Romans 16 is taken as connected to the Roman letter and intended for the Roman people, it becomes quite clear that we are speaking of a substantial and influential group of Christians. Rome, as a capital city, bustles with movement, trade, and commerce. Such a city would not be able to contain all the believers in one meeting place. This list of greetings appears to contain at least four distinct house churches. For the majority of society the fictive kinship groups that develop in the early church are not the norm. This text exemplifies the new gender, ethnic, and class relationships that are formed as Christian communities are developed.

We have much to learn from this list of greetings. Yet first, in order to get the broad picture, one needs to place it within the context of the whole book. We will study the letter in the hope of extrapolating information about the readers, how they related to one another, and what issues the letter highlights for their attention.

Roles within the Community

In addition to location and ethnicity one must also consider the roles played by the variety of believers who make up this list. It is possible that some husband and wife teams are located in this list in addition to

Prisca and Aquila. It is probable that both Andronicus and Junia (16:7) and Philologus and Julia (16:15) were partners, as their opposite gender names are connected with the conjunction *kai* (and). There are other familial ties suggested, for example, Tryphena and Tryphosa (16:12), whose names are similar in sound and form, and who may have been sisters. Rufus (16:13) is mentioned with his mother, and Paul refers to her as being a mother to himself as well. Nereus is greeted along with his sister, who is not named (16:15). It is clear from the language used in this list of greetings that family ties, whether biological or fictive, are important within these church communities.

Connections exist between these people and the community from which Paul is writing. At the end of the greeting list he tells them to greet one another with a holy kiss, and that all the churches greet them. These Christians had relationship ties with believers beyond the bounds of Rome.

In Romans 16 we read of males and females in a variety of church leadership positions. Phoebe was a deacon at Cenchreae near Corinth, a patron, and probably the bearer of the letter. We read that she was "being" (present tense participle) a deacon, implying that she was currently in leadership at Cenchreae. The questions come when we ask about what a deacon did in the early church. Why was Phoebe not called a "deaconess"? Was her role limited to caring for women? It seems that at this stage in the early church there is no diaconal office. The order of deaconess had not been formed by this stage, as the word *diakonissa* did not come into usage until the second century or third century.[21] A deacon is a servant or one who helps, and in this case, one who serves the Lord.

It seems evident from Paul's language that Phoebe is being recommended to the church at Rome. In some of the text's scribal glosses it is noted that Phoebe, a deacon from Cenchreae, brought the letter to Rome.[22] It was unusual for Phoebe, a woman, to be traveling on her own. No male kin is noted, and in the ancient Mediterranean this practice was not common. Had Phoebe obeyed cultural norms, she would have always been accompanied by a man from among her relatives. Perhaps there is evidence here to suggest that Christian women in the first century had more freedom than their pagan contemporaries and certainly more than Christian women in the centuries that followed. Yet Phoebe may have been at an advantage, as she is called a *prostatis*. This word is not well attested in the Greek literature of that time period, and appears just this once in the New Testament.[23] It has the meaning "patron" or "sponsor." She may have been sponsoring Paul on some of his missionary journeys, and she may have gone to Rome to advance the cause of his upcoming Spanish mission, a thesis suggested by Robert Jewett.[24] Clearly, she was a woman of means and influence who had leadership responsibilities in the church at Cenchreae.

Prisca and Aquila hosted a church in their home. They worked together to advance the cause of Christ with Paul as a coworker. Others worked hard for the Lord also. There were apostles, coworkers, and leaders in the church who worked side by side with Paul to advance the cause of Christ in first century Rome. This text exemplifies the variety of roles played by sisters and brothers of the faith, roles that do not appear to be determined by gender, ethnicity or class.

Ethnic Diversity

To more fully understand the audience from within the text, one also needs to look for evidence of relationships between these diverse groups in the letter as a whole. The clearest distinction in ethnicity is between Jew and gentile. In the first chapter we are told that salvation has come first to the Jew and next to the Greek (1:16), and in the next chapter that God does not discriminate but treats both groups without partiality (2:9–11).

The law, which would have been well known to the Jews, is discussed throughout the letter, but initially in 2:12–16. They are told to be not only hearers of the law but also doers. The gentiles are able to follow the law even though they do not have it (2:14). The law should now be written on their hearts (2:15). They are warned that being Jewish does not mean that they can assume to know God's will. Verse 23 reminds the Jews that they also break the law, and verse 27 makes clear that even uncircumcised gentiles who keep the law will condemn Jews who do not abide by it. We come to understand that circumcision is no longer a physical act, and thus only for the Jews, but is now a spiritual or internal symbol.

The comparison of Jews and gentiles continues. The advantages of being a Jew are outlined, and yet all people are said to be under sin—all have fallen short of God's glory (3:23). Paul speaks in the third person, saying, "We hold that a person is justified by faith apart from works prescribed by the law" (3:28). The law is not overthrown by faith; rather, it is upheld (3:31). Thus, though ethnic differences do exist, we hear a clear exhortation that they are not to divide Christians.

In chapter 4, to further illustrate the point, Paul points to Abraham and David, both of whom received God's righteousness through grace, not by works. Obviously, the Jews would know these stories, and yet it does not appear to be written to them alone. More Jewish traditions are highlighted in chapter 9, where Paul mentions promises to Sarah and Rebecca and refers to the hardening of Pharaoh's heart. This dichotomy of calling to both Jew and gentile is evident when Paul speaks of "including us whom he has called, not from the Jews only but also from the Gentiles" (9:24). Scriptures from Hosea and Isaiah refer to salvation for the remnant in Israel as well as for others outside of Israel (the gentiles). In chapters 10 and 11 Paul again addresses salvation for both Jews and gentiles as he uses the illustration of the gentiles being grafted into the tree of God's family.

All this internal evidence would indicate that Romans 16 accurately depicts the diversity found in the letter of Romans as a whole. The Jewish and Greek congregations may have been mixed or separated, but clearly they were experiencing some difficulties. There were tensions between them, particularly if some were holding onto the law and were not living according to the freedom that Paul claimed belonged to them in Christ.

Evidence of Tensions

The tensions just described could have developed as a result of the Jews being expelled from Rome and then later migrating back. Yet other conflicts and tensions also appear present in the Roman church during this time. In chapter 1 ungodliness and wickedness are identified as associated with those who are suppressing the truth. They do not honor God, and claim to be wise but really are fools. They do not follow God's truth but accept a lie.

By chapter 2 Paul begins to address the conflicts that exist in the church. The Roman believers are told not to pass judgment on others when they themselves do the same wickedness that they condemn. There appears to be a problem with faultfinding and superiority in the

Roman church. Perhaps the audience has no room to judge because they too lead lives of "wickedness."

By chapter 12 we see the reemerging theme of tensions among believers. Paul admonishes them not to think too highly of themselves. He reminds them that they are members of one body, and that each one of them is given different gifts to exercise accordingly. He exhorts them to love without hypocrisy, to hate evil and to hold to what is good, and to be devoted to one another in "brotherly" love. They are called to familial love, love that is loyal and protects honor. There is a depth to such familial love that understanding the culture highlights. They are told to honor one another and to give to the needs of the saints. They are committed to protecting the honor of the church, the family of God, at all costs.

More Controversies

Another level of conflict is evident, conflict with the authorities. In chapter 13 Paul issues a clear call to respect authorities, and there are obvious indications that the audience is being persecuted by such authorities. Thus, both levels of persecution and conflict—internal and external—form the backdrop to our understanding of the Roman church and the implications of Romans 16 for the life of the church today.

In 16:17 the topic of conflict arises again. Paul urges the audience to watch for and to avoid those who cause dissensions and hindrances, those who teach the opposite of what they have learned. The deceivers are described as satisfying their own appetites, and having smooth and flattering speech that tricks the hearts of those who are unaware. Paul's final exhortation to the Roman church is that the God of peace will soon crush Satan under their feet. Who is Satan? Is it the emperor? Is it those who deceive? These questions are easier to raise than to answer. We can say with some certainty, however, that an evil presence in Rome is causing conflict and division.

Possibility of Persecutions

We read in chapter 8 that all things work together for good for those who love and are called by God, and thus, if God is with them, who can be against them (8:28,31)? There seems to be a need to encourage these saints and to remind them of God's promises in the face of suffering.

Paul asks, "Who will bring any charge against God's elect?" (8:33). He affirms that nothing can separate them from the love of God (8:35). What would be threatening to separate them? What is happening in the Roman church that such discouragement is evident? Paul quotes Psalm 44:22, referring to God's people being put to death, like lambs being led to the slaughter. Is this psalm being used to imply current persecution? If Nero is now in power, it is evident that the Christians in Rome are beginning to suffer for their faith.

Beginning in Romans 8:17 we hear about the results of patient suffering. Perhaps, as has already been alluded to, the audience is in the midst of persecution. Paul reminds them that if they suffer with Christ they will also be glorified with him, and that the present sufferings are eclipsed by the glory to be revealed (8:17–18).

A theme of persecution continues to chapter 12, in verses 14–21. Paul tells the Roman believers to bless their persecutors and not to curse them. They are also called to treat each other similarly, letting go of pride and vindication. Paul encourages them, as best they can, to share peace with all people. He tells them to allow God to address evil and not to seek revenge for themselves, to feed and care for their enemies, and to overcome evil with good.

A picture of the Roman church is forming for us. We have men and women, slave and free, Jew and Greek all worshiping together. They serve in a variety of capacities, from deacon, to patron, to leaders of the church, to hard workers, to apostles. They are in the midst of a confusing political system where some were expelled for a time and are just now returning.

The persecution of the church did not end with Claudius's reign. It was, in fact, just beginning. Nero is reported by both Suetonius and Tacitus to have later persecuted the Christians.[25] The letter of Romans is written before these persecutions, probably during Paul's stay with the Corinthians in the late 50s. Yet these references reflect a precursor to the struggle that is yet to come and is mounting even during the time when the letter is written. Only a decade or so later, at the destruction of the Jerusalem temple, Titus intended to wipe out the religion of both the Jews and Christians. The theory purported by Tacitus is that Christians had come forth from the Jews and needed to be destroyed at the root, which was the temple in Jerusalem.[26] In 70 CE the Jerusalem temple was destroyed and the separation of the Jews and the Christians became wider. The Roman church began to grapple with these conflicts. The believers of Romans 16 present a microcosm of the larger church at Rome in the first century. They were diverse and distinct, and yet were admonished to seek unity.

A Diverse People Called to Unity

In Romans 15 Paul issues a call for the people to live in unity and to be of one accord, to have one voice to glorify God. It is evident from this basic reading of and attentiveness to the whole letter that Jews and gentiles were struggling over differences in worship and daily living. Throughout the letter they are being called to live in peace and unity. They are to not make their differences a stumbling block. They are to live in harmony, to walk with one another in the journey of the Christian faith.

In Romans 16 the readers are encouraged to demonstrate tangible signs of their common fellowship. In verse 1 they are instructed to welcome Phoebe, as she was commended by Paul to their care. Later, in verse 16, they should greet one another with a "holy kiss," a greeting mentioned in other Pauline letters.[27] Perhaps a sign of shared unity was needed, and so they are told to go out from their own house church and greet one another. Their common bond was a visible sign of unity in the developing church.

All the churches of the gentiles greeted Prisca and Aquila's church. Obviously, there was a global connection. Paul connects them with the universal church by filling them in on his plans to go to Spain and telling them about the offering he is bringing from the gentiles to Jerusalem (15:22–29). Unity is not simply about health and harmony within a particular church, but is accomplished most effectively in communion with the church worldwide. These were Christians in metropolitan Rome; they did not live in an isolated bubble. They were known by other Christians throughout Paul's circle of influence.

In 13:8–10 Paul exhorts the people to love one another and to love their neighbors as themselves. In 14:1–5 he instructs them to accept the weak in the faith, but not in order to quarrel over opinions with them. They are not to judge the weak but are to leave judgment to God. There is an exhortation in 14:6 not to allow divisions to develop around issues of the day observed for the Sabbath or of what one eats. The division between clean and unclean is not meant to bring about disagreements. No one should put a stumbling block in another's path; rather, all are called to pursue peace and to build one another up (14:13,19).

Despite a variety of different practices, the Roman Christians are exhorted to live in relationship and peace with one another. They are called to accept one another in the Lord regardless of differences of opinion, ethnicity, gender, or role. They are called to unity in the midst of their diversity.

Contemporary Application

In many respects, the church at Rome is not all that different from churches in the Western world today. We are split over denominational, cultural, and ethnic differences, some acknowledged and some hidden. Even though women today are ordained in most mainline denominations (and have been for some time), we continue to argue over the issue. It is commonly acknowledged that eleven o'clock on Sunday morning continues to be the most racially segregated hour in America. We fail to trust and show respect to our more liberal or conservative brothers and sisters. We rarely see a true mixture of social classes in any one church. We speak of unity and yet believe it can be found only in agreeing on all matters of doctrine and theology. We fail at agreeing to disagree. We fear that if we allow our distinctions to be lessened, we will lose our orthodoxy or our foundation. We fail to heed the message of Paul's text. In the church there will be differences, yet when our foundation is the message of the gospel, we are on solid ground. The church of Rome, despite its differences, had a common denominator: faith expressed in Jesus Christ crucified, dead, and risen, offering salvation to all.[28]

The church at Rome was made up of several local house churches, each probably slightly different from the other. Tension and division exist over cultural practices and beliefs. And yet, Paul calls them to unity. This call to unity often gets obscured in Romans 16 because we write the text off as a mere list of greetings, or as directed to Ephesus not Rome. In coming to the text with our presuppositions, we miss the surprises it has to offer.

Romans 16 is a wonderfully refreshing text that should not be overlooked. It informs our racial, gender, and class relationships. In the body of Christ all are one. We are not to put stumbling blocks in the paths of our sisters or brothers. Living out our salvation is about living in harmony and community with one another.

If we struggle with humility, then we need to hear this message: no one can earn God's favor. We are in right relationship with God not because of circumcision, keeping the Sabbath, or good works, but because of God's grace and God's grace alone. Perhaps if we focused more on the grace of God and less on our doctrinal and physical differences, then we might be more in step with the spirit of this letter and, indeed, with the Holy Spirit. We might begin to recognize that living in unity is not without its tensions. We might realize that the believers of Rome were divided not over major theological issues but over cultural and ethnic differences. So often we allow such barriers to hinder our cooperation with one another. Attentiveness to God's grace might teach us how to negotiate the conflict and to live peaceably with all people. Let us, with the saints of the ancient Roman church—Prisca, Aquila, Phoebe, Junia, Andronicus, Mary, Tryphaena, Tryphosa, Rufus, and the others—celebrate our differences and yet be assured that in Christ we are one in the Spirit.

Questions for Further Reflection and Discussion

1. In light of our study of Romans 16, what are the differences you see in your community and in your church family? What issues divide believers?

2. How does the church often focus more on downplaying our differences than on celebrating our distinctiveness? In what ways can we celebrate our diversity and still maintain our unity?

3. What beliefs form the core of our faith on which the foundation of unity can be built?

4. If we were truly willing to walk in the message of this text, how might our communities and churches change?

5. What do you need to do to put this message into action in your life and in your church community?

Endnotes

1. For further reading see Peter Lampe, "The Roman Christians of Romans 16," in *The Romans Debate*, ed. Karl P. Donfried, rev. ed. (Peabody, Mass.: Hendrickson, 1991); Peter Richardson, "From Apostles to Virgins: Romans 16 and the Roles of Women in the Early Church," *Toronto Journal of Theology* 2 (1980): 232–61; Florence Morgan Gillman, "The Ministry of Women in the Early Church," *New Testament Theology Review* 6, no. 2 (1993): 89–94; Elisabeth Schüssler Fiorenza, "Missionaries, Apostles, Coworkers: Romans 16 and the Reconstruction of Women's Early Christian History," *Word & World* 6, no. 4 (1986): 420–33.

2. John Chrysostom, *Homilies on the Epistle to the Romans* 31.

3. See Karl P. Donfried, ed., *The Romans Debate*, rev. ed. (Peabody, Mass.: Hendrickson, 1991). See also note 5 of this essay.

4. For more information see the discussion in Bruce Metzger, *A Textual Commentary on the Greek New Testament*, 2nd ed. (New York: United Bible Societies, 1994), 470–73.

5. Edgar J. Goodspeed, "Phoebe's Letter of Introduction," *Harvard Theological Review* 44, no. 1 (1951): 55–57; Caroline F. Whelan, "Amica Pauli: The Role of Phoebe in the Early Church," *Journal for the Study of the New Testament* 49 (1993): 72, 73.

6. See Lampe, "Roman Christians of Romans 16"; Robert Jewett, "Approaching the Cultural Diversity of Roman Churches: A Proposed New Identity as 'Beloved of God,'" unpublished typescript (January 1996).

7. Suetonius, *The Lives of the Caesars* 3.36.345.

8. Dio Cassius, *Roman History* 60.6.

9. Suetonius, *Lives of the Caesars* 5.25.53.

10. See the discussion below for specifics about the churches.

11. The possible division of the house churches might be the *ekklēsia* of Prisca and Aquila (16:5); the group greeted from Epaenetus through the mother of Rufus (16:5–13) (NB: Within this grouping could be a further breakdown since the households of Aristobulus and Narcissus are mentioned specifically.); "Asyncritus, Phlegon, Hermes, Patrobas, Hermas and the brothers and sisters who are with them" (16:14); and "Philologus, Julia, Nereus and his sister, and Olympas, and all the saints who are with them" (16:15).

12. John H. Elliot, *What Is Social-Scientific Criticism?* (Minneapolis: Fortress Press, 1993), 82, 83, 131.

13. This number counts Junia as a woman; a discussion on this apostle's gender will follow.

14. Acts 18; 1 Corinthians 16:19; 2 Timothy 4:19.

15. Acts 18:18,26; 1 Corinthians 16:19; 2 Timothy 4:19.

16. Lampe, "Roman Christians of Romans 16," 224–28.

17. John Thorley, "Junia, A Woman Apostle," *Novum Testamentum* 38 (1996): 18–29; Lampe, "Junias," in *The Anchor Bible Dictionary,* ed. David Noel Freedman (New York: Doubleday, 1992), 3:1127; Bernadette Brooten, "Junia . . . Outstanding among the Apostles," in *Women Priests: A Catholic Commentary on the Vatican Declaration,* ed. Leonard Swidler and Arlene Swidler (New York: Paulist Press, 1977); Richard S. Cervin, "A Note Regarding the Name 'Junia(s)' in Romans 16.7," *New Testament Studies* 40 (1994): 464–70.

18. Chrysostom, *Homilies on the Epistle to the Romans* 31.

19. Brooten ("Junia," 14) cites Aegidius of Rome (1245–1316) as first commentator to construe Junia's name as masculine.

20. Metzger, *Textual Commentary,* 475–76.

21. Lampe, "Phoebe," in *The Anchor Bible Dictionary,* ed. David Noel Freedman (New York: Doubleday, 1992), 5:348; Caroline F. Whelan, "Amica Pauli: The Role of Phoebe in the Early Church," *Journal for the Study of the New Testament* 49 (1993): 68.

22. See Metzger, *Textual Commentary,* 477.

23. The verbal form, *proistēmi,* appears in Romans 12:8; 1 Thessalonians 5:12; 1 Timothy 3:4,5,12; 5:17; Titus 3:8,14. See Schüssler Fiorenza, "Missionaries, Apostles, Coworkers," 426; Richardson, "From Apostles to Virgins," 239.

24. Robert Jewett, "Paul, Phoebe and the Spanish Mission," in *The Social World of Formative Christianity and Judaism,* ed. Jacob Neusner et al. (Philadelphia: Fortress Press, 1988), 142–61.

25. Suetonius, *Lives of the Caesars* 4.16; Tacitus, *The Annals* 15.44.283.

26. Tacitus, *Fragments of the Histories* 2.221.

27. Romans 16:16; 2 Corinthians 13:12; 1 Thessalonians 5:26.

28. See, for example, Romans 3:21–24; 5:8–11; 6:1–8.

CHAPTER 8

Three Women Maligned

Mary Magdalene, the Samaritan Woman, and the Woman Caught in Adultery

KAREN L. ONESTI

Today, few would doubt the importance of preknowledge when trying to understand biblical texts. Preknowledge helps us understand the historical contexts of passages, their social implications, and the status and personality of each of the individuals mentioned. But what happens when our preknowledge is wrong? What happens when we have learned to understand texts with interpretations that were based on false preknowledge? Interpreting texts and allowing them to speak to us has never been as simple as reading the text and understanding the words. We must interpret what the text meant when it was written and what it means for us today. This was hard to do for Christians in the later centuries because they were blinded by their own social context inhibiting their understanding of the social context of biblical times.

Unfortunately, we have inherited a later tradition of misinterpretation along with the biblical texts handed down to us by early Christians. This is the issue with three women who often become the topic of moralizing sermons: Mary Magdalene, the Samaritan woman, and the woman caught in adultery. They are three particular New Testament women who have been slandered in preaching and teaching. Written sources outside the New Testament have libeled them. This essay seeks to summarize the impact of such interpretive traditions that have influenced how we hear these texts today and to disabuse us from tendentious exegesis that vilifies these women without any biblical support. If the Bible is God's Word to us, then we must critique such traditions that color or manipulate the biblical text. Such interpretive histories undermine or betray the true message of the first communities who remembered these women as important participants in their Jesus stories. Although we can never fully enter into the minds of the earliest followers of Jesus or fully know the intentions of the first faith communities, I believe that God assists us whenever we search for biblical truth.

Mary Magdalene

Mary Magdalene is one of the most famous women of the Bible. Unfortunately, her fame has derived more from nonbiblical sources compounding and reinforcing error than from the genuineness of the biblical text. The faulty interpretive history has impacted even the English language. In any English dictionary the word "magdalene" refers to a reformed prostitute. Recently, an English subtitle to an opera by Puccini referred to a woman as "dressed like a magdalene," suggesting the attire of a strumpet. The adjective "maudlin" derives from "magdalene" because Mary has often been portrayed in art as a weeping penitent. In hagiography and its correlative Christian art Mary Magdalene symbolizes both female sensuality and womanly penitence. It is as if her image as a scantily dressed harlot or bare-breasted seductress has been impressed upon our collective memory. Just recently, I viewed a film on the life of Jesus in which Mary Magdalene is once again portrayed as a prostitute. But it is unfair to censure Hollywood for distorting the Bible when they are merely following the Western interpretive tradition.

Mary is one of the few women mentioned in all four Gospels. She is associated with Jesus as one who follows him from Galilee in the early days of his public ministry. Mary remains faithful to Jesus, as evidenced by her presence at his crucifixion, burial, and resurrection either alone or accompanied by other female companions. Although all three Synoptic Gospels mention that women came to anoint Jesus' body after his crucifixion, Luke names them in order as Mary Magdalene, Joanna, Mary the mother of James, and other anonymous women. Mark always places her name first among other women mentioned. In Matthew and in Mark's traditional ending the women informed by heavenly messengers are witnesses to the empty tomb, but in John's Gospel Mary meets the risen Jesus, who sends Mary to tell his brothers that he is ascending to the Father. In the Johannine account Mary recognizes the risen Lord from hearing him speak her name. Mary calls Jesus "my teacher," a designation preserved in Aramaic and transliterated in Greek, establishing their relationship as that of teacher and disciple. Even if Mark's longer ending is a harmonistic addition imported from another Gospel, the cumulative evidence of all other evangelists marks Mary as the faithful disciple and witness to the resurrection.

Mary is described by the word "Magdalene," relating Mary to her home city of Magdala, meaning "a city tower." This city is identified in Greek with Taricheae, "City of Fish Salting," and is thought to be the "City of the Tower of Fish" identified in the Talmud. This bustling city was located in Galilee between Nazareth and Jesus' base of ministry, the seaside town of Capernaum. The city of Magdala had its own aqueduct and a stadium, suggesting the city's importance as the district's administrative center until the more recently founded city of Tiberias superseded it. Mary was the only disciple of Jesus to have come from Magdala. The fact that Mary could follow Jesus from the Galilee without regard to family ties suggests that she belonged to a sociological category attracted to the Jesus movement. No evangelist identifies Mary Magdalene by any familial bond. She is not associated with a husband, nor is she the mother of children or called the daughter of her father. In the ancient Mediterranean world the identity of women was usually established in relation to their fathers, husbands, or sons. The women who followed Jesus and became part of the Jesus movement were often unattached. Frequently, they were widows, divorced, or perhaps slaves. Under Roman law slaves could not legally enter into marriage. Despite whatever status Mary from Magdala might have had—divorced, single, or property of an owner—it is not her status but her character that has been demeaned by the history of interpretation.

Mary, the one from Magdala, has, unfortunately, been wrongly associated with prostitution in Christian preaching and teaching. This Mary, one of the five or six Marys of the New Testament, is falsely known to be a public sinner in the Western Christian tradition. This is in stark contrast to the Eastern Church Fathers, who referred to her as a virgin. The confusion in the West comes primarily from a series of homilies of Pope Gregory the Great (540–604). Although Gregory is famous for his introduction of the plainsong in worship, his concept of the pastoral office, and his missionary zeal to the English (likening the Angles to angels!), we will direct our attention to Gregory's exegesis. Despite his great contributions to Christianity, his faulty exegesis of mistaken identity has perhaps forever tainted Mary's reputation, damaging her image as a disciple and as apostle to the apostles. How can one man's erroneous interpretation adversely affect so many?

Gregory has been celebrated for many long-lasting innovations to Christianity and for the political acumen that earned him the agnomen "the Great." The Venerable Bede has canonized Gregory's wisdom in the *Ecclesiastical History of the English People,* in which Gregory counsels Augustine of Canterbury not to establish any new sacred places, but rather to consecrate former pagan holy sites to the triune God. For more than a millennium this cultural or religious accommodation helped set the tone for Christian missionary activity across religious and cultural boundaries. But what Gregory did in associating Mary of Magdala with Luke's unnamed sinful woman who anointed Jesus was to set the stage for Magdalene interpretation in the West for the next fifteen hundred years. It is unclear why Gregory would make such a biblically inaccurate association between these women. Yet, despite the lack of textual support in any Greek or even Latin biblical manuscript, Gregory's series exercised tremendous influence on the history of exegesis in regard to Mary of Magdala.

Part of the confusion arose from the telling of the few instances of women anointing Jesus. There may be doublets of reminisces in the Gospels. Some scholars have suggested, for example, that the feeding of the four thousand men and the feeding of the five thousand men are doublets in Matthew and Mark. Matthew reminds his readers that the count did not include the women and children who also received their fill of the loaves and fishes. In the case of Mary Magdalene, she was confused with both Mary of Bethany and the unnamed woman who anointed Jesus. Although Greek commentators generally kept these three women separate, some early bishops and teachers conflated the number of the anointings or the women involved. What is to be noted is the Western tendency to harmonize texts, to give names to otherwise unidentified persons, and to resolve any supposed conflicts between varied Gospel accounts.

Once this conflation entered the teaching tradition of the church, it was harder to hear the texts without making prior assumptions or confusing the identities of these women. Mary of Magdala comes to the tomb to anoint the body of Jesus. According to the Fourth Evangelist, Mary of Bethany anoints Jesus' feet. In Mark's Gospel the unnamed woman at Simon's house in Bethany pours ointment on Jesus' head. Luke informs Theophilus of the account but describes this same woman as a sinner. Centuries later Gregory the Great made the false connection identifying Mary of Magdala with the sinful woman who anointed Jesus, as well as conflating her identity with Mary the sister of Martha, who also anointed him. This erroneous tradition in the West took such hold that by the ninth century it was believed that Mary Magdalene, together with Martha and Lazarus of Bethany, had moved to what is now southern France. This local and popular expression of piety had no ancient biblical or historical basis, but resulted in a strong regional tradition. Sadly, the liturgy for Mary of Magdala on July 22 was also adversely affected by the accumulation of false inferences. In the sixth century, when it was popular to portray penitent harlots, hagiography featured legendary female saints whose conversion was exemplified by self-denial and austerity. As one scholar relates, about this time the Gospel reading from Luke for the feast day for Mary of Magdala wrongly identified her with the unnamed sinful woman. Moreover, other Scripture selections for her feast featured women of the streets. Such liturgical conflation of texts helped to authenticate the wrong associations of Mary as a prostitute rather than a faithful disciple and the apostle to the apostles.

By far the most damaging factor has been the production and reproduction of inaccurate Bible commentaries and other written works based on untrue sources. After the Bible, perhaps the most widely translated Christian work is the fifteenth-century *Imitation of Christ* by Thomas à Kempis. In this classic of Western spirituality Mary Magdalene is also wrongly associated with Martha of Bethany: "Did not Mary Magdalene instantly rise up from the place where she wept when Martha said to her: 'The Master has come, and calls for thee?'" This classic, read by Catholics and Protestants alike, perpetuates this false association.

Although the above-cited traditions emerge from the Roman Catholic church, Protestants have also gotten the wrong impression of Mary of Magdala because of unsound reasoning—namely, guilt by association. Because a midrash or Bible commentary on Lamentations 2:2

contains a single negative reference to the city of Magdala's fall being due to moral corruption, some have used this to substantiate the false assumption that Mary was somehow typical of her city. According to this reasoning, Mary becomes a licentious woman. A scholar as exceptional as J. B. Lightfoot took this to mean that the city was destroyed for harlotry. This has impacted our traditional conception of Mary of Magdala as a harlot herself. This midrashic criticism of Magdala/Taricheae can be offset by an equally authoritative Jewish tradition that tells of the great piety of this city, whose monetary gifts to the Jerusalem temple were so numerous that the offering had to be brought by cart. All this confirms that traditions are selective but not always discriminating, and are by their very nature cumulative. It is difficult to disabuse Christians of their long-standing misconceptions of Mary's so-called shameful past.

An additional reason for Mary's perceived negative character springs from a misunderstanding of Luke's singular reference to her as having been freed of seven demons. Of the cases of demon possession in the Gospels, only two women, Mary and the daughter of the Syrophoenician woman, fit this category. Whether male or female, nothing indicates that such people were evil and therefore possessed. Jesus heals rather than forgives those harassed by demons. In fact, in every case of demon possession, persons were healed by Jesus (in the Gospel accounts) or by the apostles (in other New Testament writings). In the ancient world sickness was often identified with the action of demons; each illness was associated with a particular evil spirit. In no case in the New Testament is there any connection between demon possession and immorality. Unfortunately, by the fourth century Jerome, in his letter to Marcella, identifies Mary as "having the seven demons of sin." In accordance with ancient ideas of interpretation of numbers, the Bible uses the number seven to suggest completeness. Unlike Jerome, who takes Mary to be full of sin, Luke's statement refers to Jesus completely healing her. Jesus' ministry as interpreted by Jesus himself through the words of Isaiah included healing the sick as much as forgiving sinners. It has been difficult to stem the tide of misinterpretation to refute figures such as Gregory or Jerome. Some have argued unsuccessfully against the interpretive tradition. Jacques Faber in 1517 and again in 1518 was the first to argue critically against the portrayal of Mary Magdalene as sexually promiscuous. Basing his work on the biblical text without recourse to tradition, he was found to be out of step

KAREN L. ONESTI **109**

with the church. Unfortunately, shortly thereafter the Sorbonne condemned him for heresy. Traditions of interpretation had become so rigid that the church became inflexible even in the face of serious study of the biblical text itself. This inflexibility was coupled with fear of "innovations" by Protestant reformers, which together reinforced such traditional interpretations.

Does a tension exist between Peter and Mary Magdalene? In the New Testament there is dissension over who is the most important in the kingdom of God. Even within the book of Acts the ministries of John and Jesus are not always considered complementary. Priscilla, Aquila, and Paul properly initiated Apollos and the Ephesians into the Jesus movement, who previously had known only the baptism of John. Sometimes the tension exists between Peter and Paul. Conflict between Peter and Paul is resolved later in Acts where James's authority remedies the controversy over gentiles becoming Christian without first converting to Judaism. A late admission of ambivalence can be found in Second Peter, that some of the things Paul wrote were hard to understand and that some people misconstrued them to their own harm. Even outside the New Testament there may be evidence of such communal tensions from traditions that circulated but were not included in the canonical texts. Gospel writers did not expect us to have but four versions of Jesus' story or presume their own accounts to be exhaustive. John admits as much, stating that not everything Jesus said and did is written in his book. Early works outside of the Bible are not always accretions but sometimes the continuance of an earlier tradition that was excluded for polemical reasons. Both Peter and Mary of Magdala could be seen as preeminent in the Gospel accounts.

In the Johannine tradition Mary is apostle to the apostles; in the predominantly Jewish Matthean community Peter receives the keys to the kingdom of heaven. Just as Peter, James, and John form the inner circle of male disciples, Mary Magdalene and Mary and Martha of Bethany are numbered among the inner female circle. Yet there remains a tension between Mary of Magdala and Peter. In noncanonical Gospels and writings, many of which are Gnostic in origin or tendency, Mary and Peter predominate. These texts often build on traditions common to the New Testament. In the *Pistis Sophia,* an early-third-century writing, Mary Magdalene poses questions to Jesus. Her preeminence is shown by her great desire for the kingdom of God.

Her heart is set on knowledge beyond all her brothers as she continues to ask the Lord for wisdom. Other second- and third-century texts that highlight the role of Mary Magdalene are the *Gospel of Thomas, Gospel of Peter, Secret Gospel of Mark, Sophia of Jesus Christ, Gospel of Mary,* and *Dialogue of the Savior,* among others. The second-century anti-Gnostic *Epistula Apostolorum* also mentions Mary as the one whom Jesus sent to tell the disciples about the risen Lord. In general, works outside the New Testament know that Jesus loved Mary beyond all the other disciples. She is called blessed among women and superior to all followers of Jesus. Her closest competitor is Peter, who vies with her for superiority. Whether in Gnostic, anti-Gnostic, or New Testament literature, Mary remains the faithful disciple of Jesus and the witness par excellence to his resurrection.

Sometimes an omission can be just as helpful in gaining insight into early Christian communities. In our discussion of Mary Magdalene it is important to assess any Pauline traditions about Mary. In 1 Corinthians 15:6–8 Paul omits the women, and Mary Magdalene in particular, from his list of those who saw the risen Lord. According to the requirements of apostleship as described by Luke in Acts, the person to replace Judas needed to have been with Jesus and his followers from the beginning and a witness to all things. Given Luke's view, we can only wonder why Paul omits Mary as a witness. One possibility is that Paul was unaware of this tradition. Paul's basis for his apostolic authority rested on his vision of the risen Lord. Paul's troubles for gaining acceptance as an apostle "untimely born" stemmed in part from his vision of a postascension Jesus as authenticating his call as apostle to the gentiles. Perhaps this is why in Galatians and Ephesians he prefers the term "revelation" of or about Jesus Christ. It is worth noting that Paul lists only men in his "official" list in 1 Corinthians 15. A second, greater possibility is that Paul omitted Mary Magdalene by choice. In the ancient world a Jewish woman was not considered a proper formal legal witness unless her testimony was substantiated by whatever man had control over her sexuality, be it her father or husband. This may explain why Paul lacks what all four evangelists attest, that the women, and Mary Magdalene in particular, were present at the tomb.

For the Gospel writers, Mary Magdalene is the faithful disciple of Jesus before and after his death and becomes the faithful witness to his resurrection. There is no biblical evidence that she was a whore or engaged in lewd conduct. Nowhere in the New Testament is there anything to substantiate that she was more sinful than anyone else. Scandalously, Mary has been romanticized in art to please the lustful eye of Renaissance men. She has been allegorized to represent female sexuality as somehow sinful. Because of this, the Mary Magdalene of the New Testament has eluded us. We must counteract a long tradition of misinterpretation instantiated by medieval conflation of penitential hagiographies, by archetypal Renaissance representations of Mary the harlot, and still evidenced today by Mary Magdalene as presented in book and film. We need to reclaim the biblical view of Mary Magdalene—faithful disciple and the apostle to the apostles—both to confirm her faithfulness and to affirm the biblical witness.

The Samaritan Woman

Unlike Paul, John is not reluctant to have women testify about Jesus. John's Gospel features the testimony of another woman. The Samaritan woman who returns to her village and convinces others to believe in Jesus is another woman maligned by the interpretive tradition without support of the biblical text. The story of the Samaritan woman who comes to the well to draw water has long been a favorite of the Christian preaching and teaching tradition. Unfortunately, in the history of interpretation this Samaritan woman is often characterized as a paramour. Contemporary sermons take her as representative of today's serial marriages: she has had five husbands and now lives with a man who refuses to marry her. Strictly speaking, the biblical account of her encounter with Jesus is not intrinsically about women who cohabitate without the benefit of marriage. This text is about believing in Jesus. It is unusual that the pericope features a woman who is also a Samaritan. Rather than accentuate difference, that this woman—a Samaritan, no less—comes to believe in Jesus, John makes her paradigmatic for every believer. The reign of God embraces all. John uses Nicodemus and Thomas as paradigmatic doubters, and Martha of Bethany and the Samaritan woman of Sychar as exemplary believers. Jesus encounters this Samaritan woman and reveals that he is the Messiah, an equivalent to the promised Samaritan Restorer, another prophet like Moses. Her faithful testimony to those in her town is as crucial to John's Gospel as Peter's profession of faith is to Mark's.

How much can we assume about Samaritan ways from Jewish ways? Actually, the distinctions between Jews and Samaritans have been overemphasized because of their own rhetoric and their mutual historical enmity. Samaritans were not as different from Jews as the Jews or the Samaritans would have us believe. Sociologically, it is a matter of sibling rivalry: closeness with difference. The more similar the religion, the greater the friction; the closer the affiliation, the more intense the conflict. We might compare two later analogous situations existing between Christianity and Judaism. Polycarp, the ante-Nicene bishop, in his Pascal Sermon blames the Jews for killing the Lamb of God; John Chrysostom in the fourth century excoriates Christians for worshiping in the city's synagogues. A more recent historical example of religious sibling rivalry might be the sixteenth-century Lutheran reaction to Anabaptist groups. It is true that the Samaritans recognized as Scripture only the Pentateuch, those first five books of the Hebrew Bible known as the Torah, or Law; nevertheless, the Jews and Samaritans had much in common. Although the derivation of the name "Samaritan" comes from "Keepers of the Law," "Israelite" is their own self-designation. Even today, a dwindling Samaritan community has accepted the practice of Samaritans marrying Jews. Certain Jewish ideas about the Messiah parallel the Samaritan expectation of a Restorer. In the Samaritan woman's encounter with Jesus she finds in him the promised Messiah or Restorer. Jesus reveals to her that the nature of the reign of God is to minimize the differences between Jews and Samaritans.

Hebrew law codes and first-century oral traditions set forth in later Jewish writings such as the Mishnah determined the inherent rights of women. These rights were based on whether she was the property of a man—her father in the case of an unbetrothed virgin, or her husband as his sexual chattel to bear sons. The bride price was lower for women who either were not virgins or who could be expected not to be virgins. An example of the latter is women who had been slaves after the age of three, who were not considered virgins even if they were still physically intact. It was believed that the hymen would grow back if a man sexually used a girl before the age of three. The value of a woman was based on her sexual usefulness to bear sons for her husband. For this reason the account of the childless Hannah and her husband, Elkanah, in 1 Samuel is all the more touching. Elkanah's affirmation of his love for Hannah is expressed in the words "Am I not worth more to you than ten sons?" Although this text is not part of the Samaritan Bible, Samaritans and Jews—Israelites both—would have shared a common worldview and upheld similar values regarding gender relations; ethnic or religious aspersions notwithstanding.

Deuteronomy, a source for Jews and Samaritans both, lists the rules for Israelite divorce as a unilateral procedure for a husband to divorce his wife. An Israelite wife who was divorced without her say also lost what she brought into the marriage. After the time of Jesus, as codified in the Mishnah, the dowry went to the bride at the husband's death or at the time of divorce. Sometimes a divorced woman returned home, if her father would have her. Since fathers were not compelled by Jewish law even to feed their own daughters, taking a daughter back was problematic. Unlike the unprotected divorced women of Israel, Roman women took what was theirs at divorce. Even the Roman orator and politician Cicero had to borrow money from his friends to recoup what he had spent of the dowry of his wealthy wife, Terentia, before he could divorce her. Jewish tradition suggested that a woman could be married only three times. The Samaritan woman surpassed this limit, which may have been John's way of suggesting the Jews' low estimation of Samaritan religion. Few have considered this as a slur arising from sibling rivalry, but many have looked with contempt upon the Samaritan woman for her marital history.

Most commentators take her statement that she has no husband as an admission of her sexual promiscuity. Jesus commends her for her truthfulness: she has had five husbands, and the one she has now is not her husband. She in turn acknowledges Jesus as a prophet for knowing so much about her personal life. Nearly all commentators see in this a psychological ploy to be evasive. Next, she questions Jesus about the proper place for worship. Commentators view this as her changing the topic, an avoidance of her guilt. In so doing, they say, she tries to refocus Jesus' attention away from herself and onto the general religious conflict between Jews and Samaritans. This traditional exegesis hides the importance of a Samaritan and a Jew, a man and a woman, discussing worship and the theology of the reign of God. John's text is not about cohabitation; rather, it parallels and contrasts the Samaritan woman's encounter with Jesus with that of Jesus and Nicodemus. Whereas the prominent Jewish leader Nicodemus comes to Jesus by night, the Samaritan woman, little valued by the Jews or perhaps by the man who refuses to marry her, meets Jesus at high noon. Traditional commentators miss this contrast by interpreting the timing of noon to indicate that the women of her community shunned her. Typically, women would have come to carry water early in the morning or in the cool of the day. Commentators often admit that this woman traveled some distance to get to this particular well. The text does not disclose that the water is better or that the religious and historical significance of the well as Jacob's well is why she makes a less convenient trip. Rather than the well water, it is the living water capable of meeting her spiritual need that evokes our attention. John emphasizes that this woman can discuss with Jesus the very theological issues perplexing Jews and Samaritans. Though Jesus speaks from a Jewish point of view, his words reflect the coming reign of God for all—Jews and Samaritan alike. When Nicodemus came to Jesus by night, he was not evading his need for being born again by questioning the impossibility of returning to his mother's womb, nor do commentators generally suggest that he was. In the case of the Samaritan woman, however, the text has been overlaid by our culture, our morals, and our "traditioned" point of view. As a result, she is usually condemned for divorcing her husbands and for living with a lover. Even her witness has been misinterpreted. She couches her testimony as a negative question: "Come and see a man who told me everything I have ever done. This one is not the Messiah, is he?" Her language establishes her as a woman who is modest or reserved. Her words do not presume upon her male listeners but invite them to believe. The wording suggests the place of women in Samaritan society and identifies her as a woman who mindfully bears her testimony about Jesus to such a society.

Again, commentators have held her responsible for the sin of divorce. But that a woman such as she had any say about divorce is out of the question. It is true that she had freedom to marry or not after her first marriage. Again, marriage was a way of life for women in the ancient world, providing them with protection and a limited legal standing. Jesus' ruling on divorce in Matthew was harsh on men, not on women. Divorce tends to impoverish women and children. This still holds true today. In Jesus' day the more liberal view was that Jewish men were the ones who could divorce, if for no other reason than they found another woman more beautiful. The conservative view held that a man could not divorce his wife except for some sexual misconduct on her part. In either case a Jewish wife had no say in preventing divorce. She could perhaps postpone its effective date through an agent, but her husband's decision to divorce her was binding nonetheless. If this Samaritan woman had no legal power to prevent divorce, it may be conjectured that her value as a woman decreased with every marriage—so much so that the man she was living with now did not even have to marry her. This tragic possibility reinforces Jesus' view, which places him among the conservatives in his stand against divorce.

His position shocked his male disciples, as related in the Gospel of Matthew, written for a predominantly Jewish Jesus community. They replied that if husbands had only the same standing as a wife in marriage—that is, no option to divorce—then it would be better not to marry. Mark, writing for a gentile community, had to apply Jesus' words against divorce in the case of gentiles. Roman freewomen as well as freemen had the legal right to marry and to divorce. Roman marriage was a contract that could be broken at will by either party, similar to today's no-fault divorce. In the Gospel of Mark, Jesus tells women not to divorce their husbands. This background assists our understanding that this Samaritan woman was no Roman citizen; she was legally a passive party. Proof of this may be deduced from the text. Jesus never chides her for cohabitation or for her serial marriages. Jesus never offers her forgiveness for any sin, nor does she show any sign of repentance before or after she believes in Jesus. What is remarkable in the text and usually overlooked is that Jesus agrees to engage in theological discussion with a Samaritan—and a woman, at that.

John's Gospel relates that Jesus' disciples were shocked to see Jesus talking with a woman who was not an acquaintance. It must be remembered that John refers to Martha and Mary as friends of Jesus, and Mary of Magdala calls Jesus "my teacher." Women and men lived in different social worlds. Mediterranean values for men and women were as different as honor and shame. In Jesus' day Herod's temple was divided into several courts, separating Jews from gentiles and men from women. The court of the gentiles was open to all God-fearing gentiles and to Jews. A wall separated this section from the court of the women. A dividing wall also separated the court of the women for Jewish women from the court of the Jews that was for males only. Gospel accounts reveal that Jesus never teaches in the court of the Jews, but is found either teaching or healing in the court of the gentiles or more often in the court of the women. This division of the sexes in Jewish temple worship was never mandated in the Hebrew Scriptures. The pattern for the tent of meeting shown to Moses had three sections. The outer section separated all the Israelites from the priests inside, and the inner section where the priests served in their daily rounds encompassed an innermost section, the holy of holies, reserved for the high priest on the Day of Atonement. Herod's temple marks the lowered status of women during the era of first-century Israel. This makes it all the more remarkable that Jesus talked with women. Jesus' refusal to allow the laws of ritual purity and Sabbath restrictions to separate him from people in need probably facilitated his interaction with women. Just as the woman with a flow of blood did not contaminate Jesus, but was blessed and healed by him, this Samaritan woman did not put Jesus at risk by interacting with him. As recorded by John, Jesus even befriended women such as Martha and Mary. These sisters lived in Bethany, a town whose Hebrew name means "Village of the Poor." To his male disciples' embarrassment, Jesus not only visited Poortown to be with women friends but also discussed theology with an unfamiliar woman from Samaria.

The interpretive tradition has in every age demeaned this woman instead of seeing her as a valiant evangelist to her Samaritan neighbors and a model for believers. Such a tradition takes her to be evading questions instead of seeking answers. Such a tradition is taken up with her marital history and her current sex life rather than her value as a woman who encounters Jesus in a profoundly personal way. Her intriguing question posed in the negative as a sign of feminine subjection and modesty has been grossly misused to counter her faith. If the early church historian Eusebius is correct that John's Gospel is, in contrast with the Synoptic Gospels, a "spiritual" one, we would do well to remember the encounter of the Samaritan woman with Jesus.

The Woman Caught in Adultery

Few passages from the New Testament intrigue our textual voyeurism as much as that of the woman caught in the act of adultery. This text is so captivating to Christians in the West that every attempt has been made to accept it as consistent with the stories about Jesus as presented in the New Testament. Despite such attempts, most scholars agree that this text was not originally a part of John's Gospel. One commentator treats the text in an appendix. The textual problems are manifest. The pericope does not exist in the earliest Greek sources. The first extant Greek manuscript that contains it dates from the fifth century. It occurs in later manuscripts, but with special markings surrounding the text. These scribal notations indicate suspicion that this section was not original. In fact, this story is a "floating" text found in several different places in two different Gospels, John and Luke. No Greek commentator for more than a thousand years mentions this text in any biblical exposition (c. 300–c. 1300 CE). In Latin the text found its way into Jerome's fourth-century Vulgate, based, as he thought, "on many Greek and Latin manuscripts." Also in the fourth century, Augustine of Hippo conjectured that several Latin manuscripts lacked this account because the church thought it to portray Jesus as overly lenient. Eusebius records that Papias, the second-century bishop of Hierapolis, gives a history of a "woman who was accused of many sins before the Lord, which is contained in the gospel according to the Hebrews." Regardless of whether this "gospel according to the Hebrews" was in Hebrew or Aramaic, it proves that the church has long sought a source for this text.

A cogent argument, based on internal evidence of syntax and vocabulary, can be made that the text belongs in Luke. This story could have circulated as part of an oral tradition, as did alternative material found in some apocryphal sayings sources, for example, the *Gospel of Thomas*. Also possible is that the pericope is a conflation of two types of stories associated with Jesus: a symbolic gesture story that needs to be explained and a pronouncement story that provides the background for a terse saying of Jesus. Despite scribal doubts, the account has been included in most translations as portraying a Jesus congruous with Jesus throughout the Gospels. Actually, the account fits the subgenre of the testing or trial of Jesus, a parallel to aretalogy in Greco-Roman literature.

The men who bring to Jesus the case of the woman caught in adultery misquote the Scripture. The law is not, as they have purported it to be, that such women should be stoned; rather, the law condemns to death both persons—male and female—involved in the adultery. Their misuse of the law makes the punishment applicable only to women: "Now in the law Moses commanded us to stone such women. So what do you say?" Jesus never resolves the case as such, but he does extricate himself from the bind of having either to contradict the law by endorsing her behavior or to misapply the law so that she alone should pay the penalty. The text's focus is not on the culpability of the woman but on how Jesus evades the test and resolves the dilemma as set up by his religious opponents to trap him. The accusation presented in the text begs the question, If they caught her in the act, where's the man? Even the prophet Nathan could go to King David and accuse him by saying, "You are the man!"

Some commentators think that this punishment was applied only to women even though the Hebrew Bible called for parity in these cases. Others suggest that perhaps her husband or betrothed enticed her to take the bait. Because the Johannine narrator exposes the motivation of the witnesses to entrap Jesus, some commentators distrust their "honesty" and see in this account a scenario similar to that of Susanna in the apocryphal book that bears her name. Given the fact that the eyewitnesses did not hale the man into court or public view, there is something amiss about the justice of the case according to the law. A few commentators, noting the purpose of the case to ensnare Jesus coupled with the missing man "caught in the act," have questioned the integrity of the witnesses and consider them not unlike the lying elders in their accusation of Susanna, the falsely accused virgin. Whereas in the intertestamental writing Susanna's reputation was vindicated and her false accusers exposed, in the Greek Testament Jesus neutralizes injustice unsupported by religious principles, while extending forgiveness: "Neither do I condemn you. Go, and from now on do not sin again." This account, whatever its original source, involves a woman engaged in illegal sexual activity. The attempt to correlate this woman with Susanna is forced, and robs the text of its import. Likewise, interpretations that focus on the sinfulness of the woman by making her a paradigm of the licentious woman miss the purpose of this text. The narrator's aim is to show that Jesus was both just in relation to the law and able to extricate himself from the machinations of his adversaries. Attempts to press beyond this usually result in a misguided variety of conjectures.

Scribes as well as commentators have variously interpreted Jesus' gesture of writing on the ground. To some, Jesus is like a Roman official writing down his pronouncement on a case. Others interpret the action of Jesus as his fixing his sight on the ground rather than looking upon a woman caught *flagrante delicto* who might have been dragged naked before the crowd. An old and interesting scribal gloss has it that Jesus was writing down the sins of her accusers. A few scholars have seen in Jesus' symbolic action a correlation between Jeremiah 17:13, where God admonishes, "Those who turn away from me shall be recorded in the earth." One view that seems to fit human psychological reactions is that Jesus was slowing down group action to make for peace. When we confront others, sometimes it is best to look them straight in the eye, but at other times to stare them down might encourage their self-justification. By looking at the ground, Jesus does not provoke them and causes them to pause. The pause stops the mob mentality and allows for self-restraint. Restraint is essential for justice, which one scholar refers to as "self-limitation," the willingness to limit our overbearing actions against others. Jesus slows down the action of the crowd to save the woman. One sociological interpretation of the text views the tendency of human communities to be based on an "all against one" mechanism of survival known as the scapegoat concept. Against this death-dealing paradigm Jesus offers a new, unifying principle, a new life instead of uprooting the sinner. Jesus would not sacrifice the woman to preserve a false sense of community holiness.

The action of this pericope, now located after John 8:52, takes place in the temple area where Jesus has taught before. The actual locus of the temple is important, even if it is simply the place where this oral tradition has found a textual home in John. Typically, Jesus is found in the court of the gentiles or in the court of the women, where the widow can offer her mite and Jesus can make his teaching available to all the house of Israel, to women and children as well as to men.

This unnamed woman has been a scapegoat in the tradition to represent supposed female sensuality and promiscuity. Whether the text is original or not, it has lodged itself firmly in the minds of Western Christians. It will be difficult for us to rehabilitate this text to represent Jesus' offer of forgiveness and his refusal to give in to the violence of the self-righteous. The Jesus of this pericope refuses to participate in the sin of violence, and we are called to follow his example. If we focus now on the woman caught in adultery, it is only to acknowledge her opportunity as our own; that is, to participate in the reign of God, to encounter Jesus, and to go and sin no more.

Conclusion

To understand these biblical texts requires much from us. Taking into account the sociological and historical contexts of these passages, the differing social implications for men and women, and the status of women in the ancient world greatly assist our proper understanding of Mary Magdalene, the Samaritan woman, and the woman caught in adultery. We engage in the profitable if demanding work of grasping what these texts were really saying about these three women in order to understand what they should mean for us today. We are no longer bound by an inherited tradition of misinterpretation. We may hear Jesus' directions about Lazarus, bound hand and foot, "Untie him, and let him go," and be freed from a history of misinterpretation. Perhaps we in turn can free the biblical remembrances of these women. Mary Magdalene, the Samaritan woman, and the woman caught in adultery are now freed once more. Freed from shame, disgrace, and humiliation, they are free to witness to the risen Lord, to inspire others to share the good news, and to teach us what God demands: mercy not sacrifice, and to walk humbly with our God by trusting in the one who can save us. As Jesus blessed Mary Magdalene, the Samaritan, and the adulteress, so God is there to help us all along the way.

Questions for Further Reflection and Discussion

MARY MAGDALENE

1. Has the image of Mary of Magdala as a prostitute or fallen woman colored how you think of her as a disciple of Jesus?

2. How important was Mary of Magdala in early Christian communities? Discuss later traditions about Mary of Magdala that reflected and/or influenced second- and third-century Christianity.

THE SAMARITAN WOMAN

1. What does it mean that Jesus reached out to women who lived in a society that considered them powerless, and offered them the choice of making a decision to follow him and accept him as revealing the reign of God?

2. Even if we adopt an erroneous interpretation about the Samaritan woman, how does this story about her and Jesus impact what we might think about single welfare moms? Divorced women who remarry and have children from their first marriage? Who are the outsiders in our faith community today? How do we include them in talking about God, that is, in theological discussion?

THE WOMAN CAUGHT IN ADULTERY

1. Can you think of times when even well-meaning people jumped to conclusions, were influenced by crowd psychology, or were dead set on committing violence? How can slowing down the action bring peace and equity? Can you give an example of when you observed how this worked for peace and resolution?

2. Can we hate the sin and love the sinner? How effective have you and your faith community been at holding to this tension? If Jesus was able to live in the tension, why do some faith communities choose the exclusion, even death, of the outsider rather than the discomfort of unclear boundaries of behavior? Does Jesus offer an alternative model short of condemnation?

3. Consider whether your faith community has ever participated in double standards for men and women, girls and boys. If so, how can you make a difference in your church community?

4. Can a faith community ever use the Bible against people? Can you give an example of someone who has been used as a test case, as was this woman? As was Jesus?

THE TRADITION

1. Do you agree with Augustine of Hippo that tradition kept the story of the woman caught in adultery out of the Bible because it portrays Jesus as being overly lenient, and it might therefore cause the church to be soft on the sin of adultery?

2. Can you think of any other traditions we hold that are not found in the Bible? If not, discuss traditions about Jesus' birth. Was Jesus born at midnight? How many magi came to see Jesus? How old was Jesus when the magi came? Where were Jesus, Mary, and Joseph living when the magi came?

CHAPTER 9

The Golden Rule and Responsibility to the Other

ROBERT L. MANZINGER

Do not seek revenge or bear a grudge against one of your people, but love your neighbor as yourself. I am the LORD. (Leviticus 19:18)[1]

You have heard that it was said, "Love your neighbor and hate your enemy." But I tell you: Love your enemies and pray for those who persecute you, that you may be sons of your Father in heaven. He causes his sun to rise on the evil and the good, and sends rain on the righteous and the unrighteous. If you love those who love you, what reward will you get? Are not even the tax collectors doing that? And if you greet only your brothers, what are you doing more than others? Do not even pagans do that? Be perfect, therefore, as your heavenly Father is perfect. (Matthew 5:43–48)

The Golden Rule: Is It about Us or Them?

Love your neighbor and hate your enemy. These contradictory statements do not belong together in the same ethical sentence. Yet they are the by-product of a long history of self-justifying ethical behavior in the Western philosophical and religious traditions of human beings aspiring to love their own people but hating others who are different from themselves. One remedy to these ethical contradictions is the mandate of Jesus to "love your enemies" (Matthew 5:43–48; Luke 6:27–36). With this mandate in mind, the purpose of this essay is twofold. First, I want to show that when Jesus tells us to love our enemies, he is sanctioning our responsibility to people different than us. Second, a Jewish ethical writer, Emmanuel Levinas, offers an analogous perspective with his interpersonal ethical relation with an "Other." For Levinas, it is the Other, someone who is singularly unique and different from ourselves, who calls us to interpersonal responsibility. The ethics of Jesus and Emmanuel Levinas will be examined in this essay because they offer us more radical versions of what is commonly perceived as the Golden Rule, both of which involve responsibility to the Other. Peace, rather than violence, is the result when we act like neighbors in our treatment of the Other and our perceived enemies. This is what it truly means to love your neighbor as yourself. Let us now briefly examine the Golden Rule, how it developed, and its treatment of people different from us.

At the heights of the ethic of Jesus are two complementary moral statements that sum up the Jewish law and prophets: "Love your neighbor as yourself" and "Do to others what you would have them do to you" (Matthew 22:34–40; 7:12). The first is the Levitical commandment from the Mosaic law, "Love your neighbor as yourself" (Leviticus 19:18), also known as the second great commandment of Jesus (Matthew 22:39; Mark 12:31; Luke 10:27). This commandment has served as an ethical cornerstone of both the Jewish and Christian religions, traditions where high ethical standards were what distinguished them from pagan religions.

The other statement, "Do to others as you would have them do to you" (Matthew 7:12; Luke 6:31), was a much later addition in ancient Judaism, nearer to the time of Jesus. This saying was usually stated in a negative form, possibly first conceived five hundred years before Christ by Confucius when he wrote: "What you do not like when done to yourself do not do to others." Negative forms of this saying were later written by Jewish rabbis prior to, or near the time of Jesus, and one such form was this: "What you hate, do not do to anyone." In a similar vein, the Jewish Palestinian Targum reading of Leviticus 19:18 combines the negative form of "do to others" as an explanation of "Love your neighbors as yourself": "You shall love your neighbor, so that what is hateful, you should not do to him."[2]

However, it is the genius of Jesus to state the rule in a positive form, "Do to others," and to connect it with acts of love, specifically, to "love your neighbor as yourself." To love your neighbor is to act like a neighbor, to do to others as you would have them do to you. Jesus connects this reciprocal action of "do to others" with the most radical form of loving your neighbor, "love your enemies" (Luke 6:27–36). The highest ethical rule known by the New Testament is to love your neighbors (*all* of them!), doing to them as they have done to you. The apostle Paul, likewise, exhorts us in our duty to love, showing the interdependence of these two sayings on loving and doing to others that combine into a single highest rule: "The commandments . . . are summed up in this one rule: 'Love your neighbor as yourself.' Love does no harm to its neighbor. Therefore love is the fulfillment of the law" (Romans 13:9–10). Seventeen centuries later—and no one knows exactly when or how—"Do to others what you would have them do to you" became known as the Golden Rule, because "golden" signifies the inestimable value of the moral principle.

The reciprocal rule of "do to others what you would have them do to you" has a variety of forms in many different religious traditions. However, Jesus clearly connects "do to others" with "love your neighbor as yourself" as the one ethical rule of inestimable value, summing up the Jewish law and prophets. These two ethical sayings are woven together into threefold strands by the Jewish *Shema* (Deuteronomy 6:4–5) or the first great commandment of Jesus (Matthew 22:37–38) to form distinctively Jewish and Christian versions of the Golden Rule.

As commonly understood, however, there are serious defects with these and other versions of the Golden Rule. The great Christian theologian Paul Tillich identified the Golden Rule as a formal ethical principle lacking the content for justice in interpersonal encounters. It is a calculating means of practical wisdom for getting other people to treat you the way that you want to be treated. As a formal ethical principle, it fails to acknowledge the other person as a person.[3] In the Levitical law, the Jewish ethical precept "love your neighbor as yourself" provided directions on how to treat fellow citizens and neighbors. It showed how to treat our people. It did not emphasize how to treat people different from us, or how to treat our enemies.

The most trying ethical issue the Golden Rule raises for me is how to gain just treatment for those people of a different race, religion, region, ethnicity, or gender. The ancient Jewish people, like most societies, had specific rules on how to treat gentiles, women, and mixed ethnic groups such the Samaritans, or how Jewish priests would relate to Israelites. Yet the good Samaritan in Jesus' parable who practiced mercy and true neighborliness to the stranger (Luke 10:25–37) and Mary, who, unlike Martha, eschewed familiar duty to learn at the feet of Jesus (Luke 10:38–42) were prime examples of persons who broke rules that discriminated according to ethnic, class, or gender distinctions while simultaneously observing the two most important commandments of Judaism. The parable of the good Samaritan and the story of Mary and Martha illustrated that genuine differences among people, between Jewish people and both Samaritans and gentiles, between priests and Israelites, and between men and women, were not to be social barriers to just treatment. At this point, it will be helpful to see how Jesus enabled a multicultural society to affirm diversity and differences through responsibility to one's neighbor, as we briefly examine the parable of the good Samaritan.

In the parable of the good Samaritan (Luke 10:25–37), a lawyer approaches Jesus with the intention of testing him about the law, and asks Jesus what he must do to inherit eternal life. Jesus turns the question back over to the lawyer, who as an expert on Jewish law, ought to know what the Jewish Scriptures say about this subject. The lawyer answers with an expanded version of Deuteronomy 6:5, "Love the Lord your God with all your heart and with all your soul and with all your strength," and Leviticus 19:18, "Love your neighbor as yourself." The quotation from Leviticus 19:18 is linked here for one of the first times with this expanded version of Deuteronomy 6:5. (In the parallel passages of the same story in Matthew 22:34–40 and Mark 12: 28–34, it is Jesus himself, and not the lawyer, who ties this first commandment of Deuteronomy 6:5 with this second commandment found in Leviticus 19:18.) In the Lukan parable, Jesus responds to the lawyer that he has answered correctly and then tells him to "Do this and you will live" (Luke 10:28). Devotional knowledge of God is linked to ethical action.

Then the lawyer asks the more challenging question, "Who is my neighbor?" The lawyer is making sure the boundary walls are still intact, so that only those who are comfortably inside of these socially acceptable boundaries may receive just treatment from him. But Jesus creates the story that illustrates anyone can be the victim of misfortune. The main character of this parable is only described as "a certain man" and not characterized by any specific region, religion, race or trade.[4] Jesus describes how this man is attacked on a mountain road, robbed, beaten, and left for dead. The priest and the Levite, the first two people to come upon the man on this road, are both expected to stop and help someone close to death. Yet neither one does, and we are given no reasons as to why they do not stop. Finally, the good Samaritan shows mercy and neighborliness. When Jesus asks the lawyer which one was a neighbor to the fallen man, the lawyer would not even admit that this compassionate person could be a Samaritan. Instead, he answers, "The one who had mercy on him," and Jesus tells him, "Go and do likewise" (Luke 10:37). The boundaries of the identifiable neighbor have been expanded to anyone in need. There is no justification for ignoring or mistreating other people, especially those of lower social status. Most importantly, however, Jesus shifts the ethical issue from identification of "who is my neighbor" to a call to be responsible to the stranger in need, the person who is much different from oneself.

Jesus redirects the lawyer's focus from identifying who is my neighbor to who was a neighbor—or who *acted* like a neighbor. If Jesus had identified the neighbor in specific terms, this would have offered justification to the lawyer to act in accordance with specific rules of socially acceptable conduct. Instead, Jesus shifts the lawyer's agenda by portraying the central character in this story, the person attacked by robbers, as a generic individual who could have been any one of his hearers. The point is not to identify and categorize your neighbor according to social conventions and then decide whether to give assistance or not, but to act like a neighbor to any particular person who is in need, as we are all called to serve. We are responsible at each moment for that particular person whom we see in need. The human face of that person is a demand placed upon us. When we see a human being in need, our response must not be avoidance, mistreatment, or violence, but responsibility.

Unfortunately, in the New Testament Gospel of Matthew, to "love your neighbor" when taken literally, as it was in Jesus' time, was commonly interpreted to mean "Love your neighbor and hate your enemy" (Matthew 5:43–48). This contradiction and tension between loving your neighbors and hating your enemies draws out a fundamental pragmatic flaw in the Golden Rule as commonly perceived: It may be used to justify hatred and violence toward one's enemies, to those who are not one's friends or neighbors. Loving your enemies, whether it was a new ethic given by Jesus, or a further amplification of the Golden Rule, was certainly not a well-practiced code of conduct then or now. There *are* a number of examples in the Old Testament that testify to reaching out to one's enemies, and the actions of the prophets Jonah and Jeremiah readily come to mind. Yet, even though there may have been no categorical injunction in the Old Testament to hate your enemies, its pages are rife with the extermination or mistreatment of Jewish enemies. The Amalekites, for instance, are a people dubbed as God's eternal enemy (Exodus 17:14), and the Israelites are told to "blot out the memory of Amalek from under heaven" (Deuteronomy 25:19). This hatred for one's enemies is not confined to the Old Testament. Angry and even violent denunciations of Christian enemies can be found in the New Testament as well, particularly in the book of Revelation. John Dominic Crossan makes the even more extreme case that Christian anti-Semitism shaped the passion narratives in the Gospels.[5] My goal here is not to document the extent of the hatred and violence to be found in the Judeo-Christian Scriptures. Nevertheless, if the Golden Rule is to be maintained as the highest ethical standard, then it must be shown that loving our enemies is what Jesus expects from us, and that violence is the result of not loving or forgiving our enemies.

At this point, I want to introduce a Jewish thinker, Emmanuel Levinas, whose contributions to ethics are valuable to this discussion. My contention in this essay is that Levinas is helpful in developing the Levitical tradition of "Love thy neighbor as thyself." Levinas advances concepts of responsibility to the face of the Other that parallel what Jesus is saying when he begins to define how to treat someone who is very different from ourselves, such as in the parable of the good Samaritan (Luke 10:25–37), or when Jesus points to the faces of the poor and the disenfranchised as bearing his own face and as those to whom responsibility is due in the parable of the sheep and the goats (Matthew 25: 31–46), and when he commands us to love our enemies, not just our friends (Matthew 5: 43–48). This radical ethic of Jesus is an ethic of risk that begins with an interpersonal relation with another person. Levinas calls this person the Other. Let us now turn to examine Levinas's central thought, the interpersonal ethical relation and its responsibility to the Other, before making some comparisons and drawing some conclusions about the ethics of Jesus and the ethical relation of Levinas.

Emmanuel Levinas and the Ethics of the Other

Emmanuel Levinas (1906–1995) is one of the most intriguing and original ethical thinkers of the twentieth century. Levinas, who was born of Jewish parents in Lithuania in 1906 and educated in France, was influenced by the biblical and talmudic texts of the Jewish tradition and by Jewish philosophers Martin Buber and Franz Rosenzweig. The culmination of his formal education came with attending the lectures of Edmund Husserl and Martin Heidegger in Freiburg, Germany, in 1928 and 1929, and with completing his 1930 doctoral dissertation, "The Theory of Intuition in the Phenomenology of Edmund Husserl." Heidegger's collaboration with the Nazis and his 1933 rectorial address in support of Adolf Hitler were a severe shock to the young Levinas. Later, as a French citizen and military officer in World War II, he was forced to labor in a Jewish work force in a German prisoners' camp, while his parents and brother were murdered by collaborators of the Nazis. Although Levinas viewed himself as a phenomenologist, I think that we are also compelled to understand his ethical thought religiously in relation to Judaism and the *Shoah* (or Jewish Holocaust).

Emmanuel Levinas highlights two foundational difficulties with the history of Western philosophical and religious intellectual traditions. The first is that he opposes the unity of the Western philosophical systems of "Being," as they inevitably become systems of violence, attacking differences and diversity. For Levinas every individual is not only unique, but irreducibly singular, a notion that he calls "Infinity." Levinas's Infinity cannot be contained by any philosophical or theological system, as it is absolutely Other; it entails a movement of alterity, or Otherness, which transcends description and human thought and occurs within an interpersonal face-to-face ethical relationship between a self and an Other. Any system that collapses all singularity into a final unity does violence to the genuine differences between people. Hence, human beings cannot be placed under some general category of what it means to be human for everyone, such as Heidegger's

Dasein, the human structure of a self "being-there" within a unified world of Being. Levinas criticizes metaphysical totalities such as Heidegger's for reducing the Other to sameness and for lacking the ethical power to stop its own violent tendencies of enforcing conformity or—in the case of the *Shoah*—enacting genocide to exterminate differences. Levinas views this Western concept of Being as a tradition of violence that engendered the totalitarian cruelty of Adolf Hitler and Joseph Stalin. The *Shoah* can be seen as the culmination of this tradition.

The second problem for Levinas is that the Greek tradition locates the beginning of both philosophy and ethics in the self or the "I." From Socrates' "Know thyself" to Rene Descartes' "I think, therefore, I am" and beyond, Western philosophy has maintained the Greek tradition of the self. Likewise, the history of Western ethics, from Aristotle's virtues to Immanuel Kant's moral rules, from John Stuart Mill's pleasures to Ayn Rand's subjectivism, has emphasized a morality that begins with the self. For Levinas—and I believe he is correct here—any ethics of the self without responsibility for the Other will not be ethics at all. (I offer two examples: Thomas Hobbes's "ethical egoism" and Ayn Rand's "ethical subjectivism.") Hence, while someone like Søren Kierkegaard would agree with Levinas's opposition to the totalizing "system" that erases differences, Levinas differs from Kierkegaard in that it is not the Kierkegaardian "I" nor the non-conformist "individual" who resists the system, but the Other who deconstructs the system of which the self is a part. Thus, Levinas counters the emphases of metaphysical systems of Being and the self in Western ethical thought with his interpersonal ethical relation and the Other.

The basis of Levinas's ethical thought is that the interpersonal face-to-face relation with another human being (the Other) is prior to everything, even one's relationship with oneself. (For Levinas, God happens within this interpersonal human relation.) He speaks of the ethical relation as a phenomenological structure of human existence. Given this structure of human existence, Levinas believes, we are born with an infinite responsibility to the Other. This is reflected by the biblical story of Abel and Cain where Cain asks, "Am I my brother's keeper?" (Genesis 4:9). The answer, of course, is that we *are* our brother's and sister's keeper. We feel this when we realize that we have an inborn sense of responsibility to someone else who is suffering and a corresponding desire to ameliorate his or her pain. This does not mean that we are responsible to everyone all at once, or that our neighbor is humanity in general. We respond to a particular Other, and I would add, the Other whom God places in our path. Levinas articulates an interpersonal ethic, of an Other to whom I respond.

Who is Levinas's Other? The Levitical law calls for equality, but the nature of Levinas's ethical relation is inequality. The Other is higher than I am, an elevation that approaches me with the face of the destitute. The visible Other has the face of the poor, the orphan, the stranger, the widow, the homeless, and those without power or protection.[6] The Other shares much in common with the list of those who bear the face of Jesus in the parable of the sheep and the goats (Matthew 25:31–46), such as the hungry, thirsty, sick, imprisoned, poor, and the stranger. Levinas's Other is not an alter ego, or another self with different properties who is otherwise essentially like me. The Other resists fusion or totalization and is unique as experienced as an Other in his or her singularity, not in individuality as in Kierkegaard's non-conformist I. Thus, the uniqueness of the Other does not refer to particular differences between people. In a metaphorical sense, singularity speaks about the invisible Other, the alterity of the other person that goes beyond human thought or knowledge. This uniqueness that cannot be expressed, Levinas calls "election," for I have been chosen not by my will or the Other's will but by the Other who reveals him or herself to me through his or her face. Levinas adds that it is the face of the Other that calls us (not just our needs as individuals), and the demand of the Other is never satisfied. For Levinas, the Other in its furthest reaches is a coming to God, but this occurs only in relation to a human Other.

This is a radical shift from the Western ethical tradition that has always begun discussions on ethics with the I, or the self. In the Western ethical tradition, we usually begin a conversation on ethics by asking the questions "What should I do?" or "Am I doing the right thing?" or as Christians "What would I do if I were Jesus?" But for Levinas, we don't know what to do (or what we would do if we were Jesus) unless we first encounter a particular person, an Other. For Levinas, we must not categorize the Other in advance by reducing his or her distinctive Otherness to our own thought patterns. If the Other is primarily something to be known, then the Other will be known and controlled through this knowledge. We are not isolated ethical subjects who know people and then do something for them. We are persons engaged in an interpersonal relation, and in that relation it is the Other who defines our identity. This is a fundamental shift not only in what we should do, but in the way that we view ourselves and other people. This basic orientation of moving toward the uniqueness of another person who comes before me in the mystery of their Otherness, rather than of a self who views and categorizes someone from within his or her own world, is a difficult concept to grasp. It is a radical notion to say that our own identity or ego only begins to take shape in relation to an Other.

However, this orientation to an Other is not a idea foreign to Christianity. Jesus speaks about the identity of the self when he says that we must follow him and lose ourselves in order to find ourselves (Mark 8:34–36), and the apostle Paul adds that, for Christian identity, "it is no longer I who live but it is Christ who lives in me" (Galatians 2:20, NRSV). The more I become responsible in following Christ's call to sacrifice my life in *agapē* love for other people, the more I will find myself in relation to God. This means that my relationship with God is even prior to my relationship to myself. Levinas is saying much the same thing about our relationship with a human Other, except that God passes by ("illeity"[7]) in the interpersonal ethical relation. For Levinas, God is found in the ethical relation, when the face of the Other calls me to responsibility.

This ethical relation that calls for responsibility to the Other has three different aspects that bear a brief explanation at this point. First, the call and command of the Other to responsibility is revealed through the face. Second, the response to the Other is governed by my passivity, as I am held hostage to the Other, in what Levinas calls "substitution." Third, the call of the face places an asymmetrical demand on the responsible self, a call that cannot require reciprocity. Each of these aspects will be examined in turn.

REVEALED IN THE FACE

First, the call and command of the Other is revealed in the face. The face of the Other is infinitely beyond the powers of comprehension. The Other cannot be grasped. This is the power of the face. For Levinas, the face is a phenomenological abstraction, and as such, he describes it in philosophical terms. However, it need not be so complicated. The visible dimension of the call is what we can ignore sight unseen, but we cannot ignore in person. When we see the face of the hungry, the homeless, the poor, when we observe their faces, we desire to do something about their condition or situation. In Levinas's thought, the practical level of the experience of the Other occurs in a face-to-face encounter. This parallels what Jesus says in the parable of the sheep and the goats (Matthew 25:31–46), namely that when we have seen the hungry and thirsty, the stranger, the poor, the imprisoned, or the sick and were responsible to them, then "I tell you the truth, whatever you did for one of the least of these brothers [or sisters] of mine, you did for me" (Matthew 25:40). Jesus calls Christians to be neighbors who respond to the call of God and the cry of those in need. However, for Levinas, we are called to this responsibility not by Jesus, but by the Other.

When we look into the face of the Other, it places a demand upon us. If some people have trouble looking into the face of the homeless person, what is the reason for this? If they were to truly look at a homeless person, then they may hear the call to responsibility that the face of the homeless person places upon them. We can talk all we want about how people all over the world are starving, but it is not until we have seen the face of a particular starving child that the point is driven home and we feel responsible. My world is disrupted by the face and the speech of the Other who appears to me from the heights as a revelation. The face is an expression, a nakedness without defense, that commands me ethically and forbids me to kill. With the tragic background of the Other in mind, the Other's command and binding call to the self can be graphically depicted as "Please, do not kill me."

GOVERNED BY PASSIVITY

Second, Levinas describes the primordial passivity of the I or the self in the ethical relation. The passivity of the self held hostage to the Other is prior to any activity, judgment, or response on the part of the self. This is my ethical constitution even before I ask "What should I do?" My existence is determined by my relationship to the Other. I am a substitute, a hostage to the Other, as I am called or chosen by her face.[8] The most extreme moment of passivity, when I am so little for myself and so greatly responsible for everything that has to do with the Other, is what Levinas calls "substitution." In this primordial passivity or substitution for the Other, I am responsible to the Other in a responsibility without limits, such that I bear his pain in my own body. Levinas is fond of quoting from Fyodor Dostoyevsky's *The Brothers Karamozov*: "We all are responsible for everything and everyone in the face of everyone, and I more than the others."[9] My responsibility to the Other imposes a burden of guilt on me that I can never pay off. In the way that the biblical prophets respond to God, so I am to respond to the Other: "Here I am."[10]

AN ASYMMETRICAL DEMAND

Third, my responsibility to and for the Other consists of an asymmetrical demand in this originary ethical relation which runs counter to the reciprocity of the Golden Rule. The Golden Rule to "love your neighbor as yourself" or to "do to others what you would have them do to you" is based on a reciprocal demand and response. My neighbor ought to treat me, or respond to my demands, in like fashion to the way that I respond to hers. However, Levinas's insistence on the asymmetrical demand means that I respond to the demand of the Other regardless of whether he responds to me. Levinas's asymmetrical demand can be viewed along with Jesus' own amplification of the Golden Rule, "Love your enemies." Jesus charges us to not repay evil for evil, and to do good and expect nothing in return (Luke 6:27–36). Levinas's ethical relation and Jesus' "love your enemies" both involve an asymmetrical demand and responsibility either to the Other or to one's enemies.

Let us briefly look at the radical nature of what Levinas has said up to this point. One might rightfully ask, if everyone is infinitely responsible for everyone else, then why not say that our responsibility for one another is reciprocal? Levinas does insist on the face of the Other presenting each of us with an infinite demand, but my response to the Other (and vice versa) is not governed by his or her response to me. In other words, our response to others in love is not governed by whether they respond in kind to us with love. We do not withhold our actions, or wait and see what others may do. We act the way we know we are supposed to act, regardless if no one else acts that way in return. Self and Other are called to respond, but neither one's response is based upon the other person's.

Levinas perceives life with the Other as an Abrahamic journey to places unknown, rather than as the duty of the Greek Odysseus who returns home after completing his military assignments. Those who follow Abraham are called to make an expenditure without the security of the return home. This means openness to alterity in the face of the Other. We are always being uprooted and decentered by the Other, and we become a different self after each encounter with an Other. My response to the asymmetry of the demand of the Other is what constitutes me as a self, not just as a subjective I or as an individual. I become a self by being hostage to the Other.

Conclusions

I want to draw some conclusions about how the ethic of Jesus and Levinas's ethical relation amplify the Golden Rule toward responsibility to the Other. I summarize some of the features of Christian responsibility, and then address how Levinas's ethical relation to the Other expands our vision for the treatment of persons different from ourselves. In the view of both Jesus and Levinas, we are to accept the demand of asymmetrical responsibility to the human face of an Other if we are to truly love our neighbors as ourselves.

I began this essay by stating that the Golden Rule, "Love your neighbor as yourself" and "Do to others what you would have them do to you," has been the cornerstone of Judeo-Christian ethics. I also asserted that the Golden Rule has pragmatic defects due to literal interpretations that allow us to hate our enemies, to mistreat people who are different from ourselves, and not to acknowledge the other person as a person. The injunction of Jesus to love our enemies counteracts the first defect of the Golden Rule—that it may be used to justify hatred and violence toward our enemies—with a positive command. Enemies are accorded the same ethical consideration as friends. Moreover, "love your enemies" places an asymmetrical demand on us to love our enemies no matter what they have done, or will do, to us. We are not to repay evil for evil in reciprocal fashion. We are to bless those who persecute us (Romans 12:14), and to be good and merciful to our enemies, expecting nothing in return (Luke 6:35). The call to love our enemies comes from Jesus, and the responsibility for meting out justice for what we think our enemies deserve is left to God.

The second defect of the Golden Rule is that it does not emphasize *how* to treat others who are different from ourselves. The parables of the good Samaritan and of the sheep and the goats address this in part, as they further extend the injunction of Jesus to love our enemies. In the parable of the good Samaritan, Jesus shifts the focus away from *identifying* our neighbors and treating them according to social conventions, to accepting responsibility for *being* a neighbor to someone in need, even a person who is much different than ourselves. I do not know whom I will meet on the road—it could be anyone. For the Christian, responsibility comes with the call from God toward a specific person, a self-sacrificial response to a human face. Jesus instructs us in the parable of the sheep and the goats to respond to the needs of the poor, the imprisoned, the stranger, and the sick, because these people bear the face of Jesus. Jesus calls us to be responsible as a way of life, informed by the lowliness and humility of a servant's attitude, and accepting the servant's life as its own reward. Furthermore, if we are living the self-sacrificial life of Christian *agapē*, our character and identity will be shaped by our response to the call of Christ to act like a true neighbor. It is then that we truly become more Christlike.

It is at this point that Emmanuel Levinas is helpful in expanding our vision of how to treat people who are different from ourselves. Levinas's concept of the interpersonal ethical relation is valuable for extending our call to the Other. Levinas describes the need to fully acknowledge the another person as a person. His ethical relation depicts the constitution of a self that is already oriented toward the Other. We are drawn to a human face, and this face calls us to a responsibility that goes beyond meeting emergency human needs. The call that commands me comes from a specific (not a generic) person even before I ask the question, "What should I do?" It is the singularity of the face of the Other that calls us. The face is a height and a transcendence, and a glorious abasement from the Other, whom society may or may not consider our equal. The face of the Other commands us from on high, and elevates us in moments of transcendence. The responsibility to the Other is infinite, not merely until the good Samaritan's innkeeper friend has decided that all physical needs have been met in full. The demands of the Other are never satisfied, and our responsibility to the Other never ends.

Some of this may sound like echoes of self-sacrificial Christian *agapē* love, so let me attempt to explain in practical terms how Levinas might restate the Golden Rule. Instead of saying that we ought to love our neighbor as we want to be loved ourselves, Levinas might say that we love the Other the way that he or she wants to be loved. Levinas might say that we treat the Other the way that he or she wants to be treated, rather than the way that we would want to be treated under similar circumstances. For Levinas, ethics begins with the Other, not with an understanding of the Other as one of my people, or as someone like myself.

However, the Golden Rule makes the assumption that we know how the neighbor wants to be treated, namely, the way that we want to be treated. It is natural for me to imagine myself in the place of other people, but for Levinas, I may wrongly assume that I know how others want to be treated—the same way that I would. How would I want to be treated if I were poor or homeless, widowed or a stranger? A reciprocity in reverse is assumed. Someone may assume that a poor woman needs money for food, but at this moment, she may need someone to listen to her because the Christmas holidays prompt memories of her deceased husband. Therefore, says Levinas, we must not assume that we know how others want to be treated. The Other is not like us. There first must be a willingness to listen to the Other, to get to know the Other on the Other's own terms, before attempts at dialogue or even self-revelation are appropriate.

Now, one caveat is in order here. To love someone the way that he wants to be loved does not mean that you support his self-destruction. It does not mean that you give drugs to the addict or money to the con artist. The longer that we actually listen to the Other, the more we will be able to discern self-destructive tendencies and lifestyles. This takes time, but we are not merely to respond to the Other's needs, as if that were the extent or the true purpose of the ethical relation. It is not merely the needs of the visible Other that call us. The heights of the alterity of the invisible Other call us to infinite responsibility in this interpersonal relation, in moments of transcendence with the divine. Furthermore, accepting responsibility to the Other in my encounter with her shapes my identity as a self.

In practical terms, Levians's infinite responsibility to the Other may seem overwhelming, much like the call of Jesus to self-sacrificial *agapē* love. Levinas's ethic supposes a healthy individual capable of tremendous responsibility, and not surprisingly, his moral hero is the saint. I would assert that there are practical limits to responsibility and that there is only so much Otherness an individual can accommodate from another person and incorporate into him- or herself at any one time. The theologian Bernard Loomer refers to this healthy acceptance and incorporating of Otherness, without destroying one's own identity as "size."[11] However, for Levinas, self is revealed within an interpersonal relation, and I cannot become a self without an Other. We cannot escape responsibility to the Other.

In sum, the ethic of Jesus and the ethical relation of Emmanuel Levinas amplify the Golden Rule by showing us that our responsibility to the face of a human Other is an asymmetrical demand that brings the love of God into the world, and that shapes the identity of both the self and the Other. There is a particularity to the Other or to the neighbor to whom we are called that I think sets practical limits to our infinite responsibility. We are not responsible to everyone all at once, or to humanity in general, as this would truly be overwhelming. There is a place for social action and political reform on a larger scale, but that issue lies beyond the scope of this essay. Our ethical *responsibility* to the Other may be infinite, but the *Other* is very particular. Being responsible to many Others distances me from infinite responsibility to only one person and destroys the monopoly of one person's demands. We start with an Other before going to another and another and another.

Questions for Further Reflection and Discussion

1. In what ways are you responsible to another person? What are some of the limits of your responsibility to that person? How does your responsibility to a second person affect your responsibility to the first person? Are your practical limits of responsibility really needs-based after all? Why or why not?

2. What do you think about Levinas's idea that God is met in the ethical relation or in the interaction between two people? What are some of the ways that God might personally meet us in this type of interaction? Are there some other ways that God may be experienced beyond the interaction of only two people?

3. In what ways does Christian self-sacrificial *agapē* love or the command of Jesus to "love your enemies" begin with the Other and not the self?

4. How does the human face reveal the singularity or uniqueness of the Other? How does it call me to loving treatment and forbid me to kill?

Endnotes

1. All Scriptures are quoted from the New International Version of the Bible.

2. Targum, "Pseudo-Jonathon: Leviticus," trans. Michael Maher, *The Aramaic Bible*, vol. 3 (Collegeville, Minn.: The Liturgical Press, 1994), 177. Cf. D. M. Beck, "The Golden Rule" in *The Interpreters Dictionary of the Bible*, vol. 2, ed. George Arthur Buttrick (Nashville: Abingdon Press, 1984), 438.

3. Paul Tillich, *Love, Power, and Justice* (London: Oxford University Press, 1954), 78–80.

4. Alan Culpepper, "Luke," *The New Interpreters Bible Commentary*, vol. IX (Nashville: Abingdon Press, 1995), 229.

5. John Dominic Crossan, *Who Killed Jesus?: Exposing the Roots of Anti-Semitism in the Gospel Story of the Death of Jesus* (New York: Harper Collins Publishers, 1995).

6. Emmanuel Levinas, *Totality and Infinity: An Essay on Exteriority*, trans. Alphonso Lingis (Pittsburgh: Duquesne University Press, 1969), 251.

7. For Levinas, illeity is not a full or even a partial presence of the divine, but a "trace" of the passing by of God (Exodus 33:20–23). Illeity only occurs as the moment of transcendence in the face-to-face encounter with another person.

8. Emmanuel Levinas, *Otherwise Than Being or Beyond Essence*, trans. Alphonso Lingis (Pittsburgh: Duquesne University Press, 1969), 113–18.

9. Adriaan Peperzak, *To the Other: An Introduction to the Philosophy of Emmanuel Levinas* (West Lafayette, Ind.: Purdue University Press, 1993), 171.

10. Emmanuel Levinas, *Ethics and Infinity: Conversations with Philippe Nemo*, trans. by Richard A. Cohen (Pittsburgh: Duquesne University Press, 1985), 106.

11. Bernard Loomer, "S-I-Z-E," *Criterion* 13 (1974): 5–8.

CONCLUSION

What can we now say about the interpretation of Numbers 25 and the idea of the Phinehas Priesthood? Does God's approval of Phinehas, who demonstrates his zeal for God by killing the Israelite man and the foreign woman he brings into the community, give us divine authority to treat those who are different from us with a similar attitude of violent intolerance? White supremacists would probably say yes, but the Bible itself seems much more ambiguous on this point.

The woman who is killed is identified as a Midianite, but she seems to be linked in some way to the Moabite women mentioned in the first part of the chapter who were engaging in sexual relations with the Israelite men and thus tempting them to engage in the worship of Moabite gods at the expense of their devotion to the God of Israel. It is true that the Moabites generally do not fare very well in the Bible. In Genesis 19 we are told that the Moabites came about as the result of an incestuous relationship between Lot and his daughter. In Judges 3 the Moabite king Eglon, who is killed by the Israelite judge Ehud, is portrayed in a most unflattering way. So the idea that Phinehas is simply trying to protect the Israelite community from the morally and spiritually degrading influence of Moabite/Midianite women seems to find biblical support, and his attitude of violent intolerance toward the Israelite man and the Midianite woman seems justified—until one considers the book of Ruth.

The book of Ruth tells the story of another Moabite woman, Ruth, who, unlike other Moabites in the Bible, is portrayed in a very favorable light. She is wonderfully devoted to her mother-in-law, Naomi, and is willing to leave her family, land, and customs behind in order to go back with Naomi to Israel and take care of her widowed mother-in-law. What is more, nobody in Israel takes any offense at Ruth's presence in Israel, and Boaz even takes her as his wife. But the author is still not finished rehabilitating the image of Moabites, for we are told that Ruth and Boaz have a son Obed, who in turn has a son Jesse, who has a son David. This makes the Moabite Ruth the great-grandmother of David, Israel's greatest king. So these people who in Genesis 19 are portrayed as having been conceived in incest are part of the bloodline of David, and, by extension, of Jesus. Why was Ruth, unlike the woman in Numbers 25, not killed when she was brought into the Israelite community? What should our response be to outsiders? Should we accept them, as the Israelites did Ruth, or kill them, as Phinehas did to the unnamed woman of Numbers 25? The biblical witness on this point is unclear, suggesting that we must be willing to dig deeper and look at this text in a less superficial way. In this brief conclusion we want to indicate how some of the reading strategies outlined in this book might be brought to bear upon the Phinehas narrative.

First we must consider the transmission of the text of this narrative. Are there significant textual variants that might influence our understanding of the text? Does this account appear in different ways in different manuscripts of the Bible? One need not know the original languages to probe this question; many English translations of the Bible include footnotes indicating divergent readings in the manuscripts. These notes always deserve close attention.

If we are satisfied that we have something close to the original text of this narrative, we must then consider whether it is relating an actual historical event and the authentic attitude of God, or whether it might be a legend developed by the later community to give divine legitimacy to the people's impulse toward violent intolerance. We saw good reason to question the historicity of the David and Goliath story. We must ask whether a similar dynamic might be at work in the story of Phinehas.

But regardless of whether this is a historical narrative or a later legend, we must also ask critical questions about its role in the church and the traditional ways it has been interpreted. As we saw in the essay on the biblical lament genre, biblical laments are a part of the church's scriptural tradition that is being largely ignored in the church's liturgical traditions. Might this also be the case with Numbers 25, and if so, why? Why do we not read a story about killing a foreigner in a liturgical setting? Cannot all Scripture be used in this setting?

Maybe we are embarrassed by this text because we do not fully understand it. As we saw in our essay about heaven, sometimes we need to go outside of the Bible to the larger historical and theological context of ancient Judaism and Christianity in order to fully understand the biblical text. Could this be the case here? What is the larger historical context in which this text was written, and how did this text function in that context? Could this text have been written at a time when the community was undergoing persecution by foreign rulers, making comprehensible the attitude of violent intolerance toward foreigners that we see displayed here?

While looking at the historical context, we may also inquire as to the social context lying behind this text. We saw how Paul's words to the Corinthians were calling for a reversal of an honor/shame social system. Might this not also apply here in an environment where honor seems to be accorded the one who acts violently instead of lovingly? If the gospel as we know it is in tension with the value system displayed in Numbers 25, what might this tell us about the nature of this text? Similarly, we saw that the diversity of the early church as it can be inferred from Romans 16 was a strength. What does this say about Numbers 25, where the overriding value system seems to be one of violent resistance toward diversity? And what do we make of the issue of gender in this text? Has the interpretation of the creation accounts affected the way women are looked at in this text? Would the reaction have been the same if the Israelite man had brought into the congregation a foreign man rather than a foreign woman? We have noted the tendency to vilify certain biblical women, such as Mary Magdalene, for no valid reason. Was Phinehas more likely to act the way he did because the one bringing foreign influence into the congregation was a woman?

Finally, how do Jesus' words about loving our enemies influence the way we read Numbers 25? Phinehas displays his devotion to God by killing the one deemed an enemy of the congregation. But the command of Jesus, as it is fleshed out in the work of Emmanuel Levinas, implies that devotion to God is linked to ethical action toward others, and especially toward those whom we define as enemies. In this context, what is the proper way to show true devotion to God, by killing our enemies or by loving them?

A multiplicity of questions can be put to Numbers 25, or any biblical text, for that matter. As we begin to engage these texts using a variety of reading strategies, we begin to gain new insights and angles of vision on them, and we begin to appropriate the subtleties and nuances contained in God's revelation to us. We think it fair to say that the white supremacist interpretation of Numbers 25 not only lacks subtlety, but also is harsh and sterile. We hope that as a result of this book you will begin to engage your mind as well as your heart when reading the Bible, and begin to appreciate the wonderful subtleties, ambiguities, and nuances that are characteristic of the way that God meets us in the Scriptures. God still speaks in a still, small voice.

GLOSSARY

apocalypse (literary genre)—a type of ancient literature characterized by dreams and visions, elaborate symbols, and a preoccupation with the end of the world and God's final victory over evil. Best represented in the Protestant Bible by the Books of Daniel and Revelation.

Apocrypha—Jewish writings, such as the Books of Maccabees, Judith, and Tobit, that appear in Roman Catholic Bibles as deuterocanonical texts, but are omitted from Protestant and Jewish Bibles.

deuterocanonical—literally, "of secondary canonical status." Used to describe books of the Apocrypha that appear in Roman Catholic Bibles but are accorded a less authoritative status than the canonical books shared with Protestant and Jewish Bibles.

feminist criticism—a method of biblical interpretation that critiques the various ways the Bible has been used to support patriarchal structures and that seeks to understand the Bible in ways that can be liberating for women.

gloss—a word or phrase interpolated into the biblical text by a later writer that is designed to render a general or ambiguous word already present in the text more specific or clear. Sometimes referred to as an "explanatory gloss."

hermeneutical grid—a set of fundamental assumptions about the nature of God, the nature of humanity, and the nature of Scripture that one brings to the process of interpreting the Bible.

hermeneutics—a philosophical discipline that seeks to understand how people derive meaning from art, literature, or life experience.

Applied to the Bible, it is the study of the interpretation of Scripture—that is, the study of how individuals go about deriving meaning from the biblical text.

historical criticism—a method of studying the Bible that seeks to reconstruct the historical circumstances that both stand behind and shape the various texts that comprise the Bible.

honor/shame—a common social system in the ancient Greco-Roman world whereby a person's chief motivation in life was to be seen both by oneself and by others in a honorable light, while doing all one could to avoid being shamed or embarrassed.

lament—a common literary genre in the ancient Near Eastern world in which the feelings of grief and despair were registered, usually in poetic form.

literary genre—a category of literature that is characterized by a particular style or function. The Bible includes such literary genres as law code, genealogy, historical narrative, poetry, prophetic oracle, Gospel, epistle, and apocalypse.

Pentateuch—the first five books of the Hebrew Bible (Old Testament), namely Genesis, Exodus, Leviticus, Numbers, and Deuteronomy. Also referred to as the Torah or Law.

Pseudepigrapha—a large corpus of Jewish religious literature, written primarily during the years 200 BCE and 100 CE. Many of the texts are falsely attributed to famous Old Testament figures such as Enoch, Abraham, Moses, and Solomon.

rhetorical criticism—a method of studying the Bible that considers the ways in which a biblical writer intentionally shaped or patterned the text for the purpose of eliciting a particular intellectual or emotional response in the readers.

Septuagint—the Greek translation of the Hebrew Scriptures (Old Testament) compiled around the third century BCE by the Jewish community in Alexandria, Egypt. Also called the LXX, the Septuagint became the Old Testament of the early Christians.

social-scientific criticism—a method of studying the Bible that employs methods from the discipline of sociology in order to reconstruct the social environment standing behind the biblical texts. Also called sociological criticism.

sociological criticism—see Social-scientific criticism.

textual criticism—a method of studying the Bible that examines the ancient manuscripts of the Bible and seeks to account for the variety of readings that occur among different renderings of the same verse.

textual history—the record of how a biblical text changed and developed during the course of its transmission over the centuries.

textual variants—the differing versions of the same biblical texts as recorded in various manuscripts transmitted over the centuries. Also called variant readings.

Torah—traditionally considered to be the first five books in the Hebrew Scriptures (Old Testament), namely Genesis, Exodus, Leviticus, Numbers, and Deuteronomy. Synonymous with the term Pentateuch in Christian usage. In Jewish tradition, however, Torah may refer to the commands and teachings of God, both written and oral.

variant readings—see Textual variants.

CONTRIBUTORS

Robert L. Manzinger received a Master of Divinity from Eastern Baptist Theological Seminary and a Ph.D. from the University of Denver, Iliff School of Theology. He has been an adjunct professor at Colorado State University, the University of Denver, and Eastern Baptist Theological Seminary. Dr. Manzinger is also an ordained American Baptist pastor serving the Mayfair Conwell Baptist Church in Philadelphia, Pennsylvania.

Terence C. Mournet received a Master of Theological Studies from Eastern Baptist Theological Seminary, and is a Ph.D. candidate at the University of Durham in England. He also has studied at the North American Baptist Seminary in South Dakota and the Anderson School of Theology in Indiana. He has served in various areas of ministry, from music and worship to preaching and teaching.

Karen L. Onesti received a Master of Divinity from Eastern Baptist Theological Seminary, an M.A. in Classics from Villanova University, and an M.A. from Temple University, where she is also a Ph.D. Candidate. An ordained elder in the United Methodist Church, Rev. Onesti has also served as adjunct professor in biblical Greek and exegesis at Eastern Baptist Theological Seminary.

Robert Parkinson received a Master of Divinity from Eastern Baptist Theological Seminary, and has contributed to the International Greek New Testament Project. He is an ordained Baptist pastor, currently serving the Lumb Baptist Church in Rossendale, England.

Julia Pizzuto-Pomaco received a Master of Divinity from Eastern Baptist Theological Seminary, a Master of Social Work at Eastern College, and is a Ph.D. candidate at St. Andrews University in Scotland. She is also associate pastor at the First Presbyterian Church of Merchantville, New Jersey, and an adjunct professor at Eastern Baptist Theological Seminary.

Robert F. Shedinger received a Master of Divinity from Eastern Baptist Theological Seminary and an M.A. and Ph.D. from Temple University. He is visiting assistant professor of religion at Luther College.

Deborah J. Spink received a Master of Divinity from Eastern Baptist Theological Seminary and an M.A. from Temple University, where she is also a Ph.D. Candidate. She is an ordained United Church of Christ pastor. She is also an adjunct professor at Eastern Baptist Theological Seminary.

Grant H. Ward received a Master of Divinity from Eastern Baptist Theological Seminary and a Ph.D. from Temple University. He is adjunct professor of biblical studies at Eastern Baptist Theological Seminary, Dean's Appointment in Intellectual Heritage at Temple University, and an ordained American Baptist pastor.

Benjamin G. Wright III received a Master of Divinity from Eastern Baptist Theological Seminary and a Ph.D. from the University of Pennsylvania. He is associate professor of religious studies at Lehigh University and coauthor of The Apocryphal Ezekiel (with Michael Stone and David Satran).